Preventing Shoplifting
Without Being Sued

Preventing Shoplifting Without Being Sued

Practical Advice for Retail Executives

Michael Craig Budden

QUORUM BOOKS
Westport, Connecticut • London

Library of Congress Cataloging-in-Publication Data

Budden, Michael Craig.
    Preventing shoplifting without being sued : practical advice for
retail executives / Michael Craig Budden.
        p.   cm.
    Includes bibliographical references and index.
    ISBN 1–56720–119–9 (alk. paper)
    1. Shoplifting.   2. Shoplifting—Prevention.   3. Retail trade—
Security measures.   I. Title.
HV6652.B83   1999
658.4'73—dc21   98–6020

British Library Cataloguing in Publication Data is available.

Library of Congress Catalog Card Number: 98–6020
ISBN: 1–56720–119–9

First published in 1999

Quorum Books, 88 Post Road West, Westport, CT 06881
An imprint of Greenwood Publishing Group, Inc.

Printed in the United States of America

∞™

The paper used in this book complies with the
Permanent Paper Standard issued by the National
Information Standards Organization (Z39.48–1984).

10 9 8 7 6 5 4 3 2 1

This book is dedicated to Connie, Heather, and Staci,
who taught me the meaning of life,

and to the memory of
Cheri Budden Dunlap,
who shared hers so well.

Contents

Preface

The taking of retail merchandise without payment is known as shoplifting. Costs to U.S. retailers from shoplifting total in the tens of billions of dollars annually. It is one of the costliest crimes directly impacting businesses. The crime of shoplifting presents a variety of challenges to retail professionals as they attempt to minimize its impact on their operations.

In attempting to deal with the problem of shoplifting, retailers find themselves fighting a major war on two fronts. First, shoplifters are stealing merchandise with a total worth that currently amounts to over $21 billion annually. Add to these billions of dollars in lost revenue and the millions that are spent trying to prevent such illegal actions, and one finds that the direct costs of shoplifting, in the tens of billions of dollars annually, is of major concern to retailers. The second front, and the one that concerns this book the most, is the potential liability attached to actions arising from the efforts of retailers dealing with the problem of shoplifting. Shoplifting suspects increasingly are suing individuals responsible for their apprehension and/or detention, and worse, sometimes are winning judgments, seemingly with alarming regularity.

In looking closely at the legal impact of antishoplifting efforts, one finds that retail stores, their employees, and others involved in the apprehension and detention of shoplifting suspects are sometimes caught between the proverbial rock (pursuing the property rights of retailers) and hard place (suits for false arrests, illegal apprehension, etc.). Store managers and others involved in the protection and management of retail inventory need to be aware of the law as it applies to their antishoplifting activities and proceed accordingly. As will be seen, the law does offer liability protection to merchants, their employees, and, sometimes, others involved in retailing who act according to the law.

The material in this book and the legal case summaries presented should not be construed to be legal advice; they are not. The information contained in this book should serve as a basis for a discussion between merchants and competent legal counsels on how best to pursue their property rights in their daily business operations. The importance of securing competent legal counsel, given that shoplifting prevention strategies and merchant protection statutes involve questions of law, is paramount.

The steps in the plan presented are paired with summaries of legal cases concerning various questions related to shoplifting apprehensions, which serve to explain the importance of each step. For those desiring a more in-depth discussion, full case discussions are available in West Publishing Company's *Reporter* series, available in law libraries and many university and public libraries possessing legal collections and from West Publishing, St. Paul, Minnesota. The author encourages those desiring more information to seek such information in the *Reporters*, as case summaries included in this text are necessarily brief. The plan used as the basis for the strategic plan presented in Chapter 1 was first discussed in "Merchant Protection Statutes: Management Safety Nets or Tightropes," by Budden and colleagues (*Journal of Managerial Issues* 3, no. 1, Spring 1991, pages 62–76).

ACKNOWLEDGMENTS

I would like to thank my parents, Rowland and Wava Budden, for instilling in their children an appreciation for education. I would like to thank my teachers at Broadmoor Elementary School, Broadmoor Junior High School, and Broadmoor High School in Baton Rouge for sharing their knowledge and skills with so many for so long. I want to thank Eric Valentine, my publisher, for his support, and David Palmer and Jackie Remlinger, for exceptional editing. Finally, special thanks to Professor John W. Yeargain for helpful research assistance, for his mentoring of my writing in the area of shoplifting law, and for his encouragement.

Chapter One

Introduction to the Shoplifting Problem

An embarrassing and potentially costly incident occurred in your store a couple of months ago. One of your employees came to you and reported that a suspicious-looking customer was walking around the store. The employee described the individual to you, mentioning that the person was dressed oddly for this time of year. The customer sported a beard and was wearing a dirty jacket. His wearing a jacket is what first attracted your employee's attention, as it was not a particularly cold day. You and the employee went to the area of the store where the customer was last seen and spotted the customer standing near a display of watches.

Once there, you observed the customer looking intently at the display. The customer then looked around but did not appear to see you. Instead, the customer moved a little closer to the display, leaned closer to the watches, and moved over in such a way that with his back to you, you and the employee could no longer see the display or the customer's hands. While you could not see what the suspicious customer was doing, you felt deep inside that the individual was up to no good. In fact, you felt very strongly that the customer was there to steal something from your store. You thought to yourself that he must be stealing a watch, perhaps several. He must have been in your store to commit a crime, the crime of shoplifting.

The customer backed away from the display, proceeded to walk up the aisle, and headed towards the front of the store. You quickly walked over to the display and noticed that some of the display slots were empty. Normally the presence of empty display slots would not alarm you, but it did at this time. Typically, when watches are sold from the display, slots are left open for a period of time, since replacement inventory, which is ordered biweekly, takes approximately six weeks to arrive. As a consequence, there are usually several empty slots on the display rack. However, as you looked at the display rack, it appeared to be missing more watches than was usual.

You turned and walked up the aisle in the direction the customer was heading. As you approached the front of the store, you noticed that the customer was now in line awaiting checkout. You watched as the customer placed a candy bar on the counter and paid for the purchase. While the clerk was counting the customer's change, the customer glanced your way and then looked back at the clerk. After receiving his change and a receipt, he picked up the candy bar, said he would not need a bag and turned to walk towards the door. As he walked away, he looked in your direction once again.

The adrenalin was rushing. You just knew this person was up to no good. Something was wrong. You felt for certain that a crime had just been committed—committed right in your presence. As the customer headed for the exit, he kept looking your way. He appeared to be stepping up his pace as he walked quickly towards the front door. You recognized the fact that in a matter of moments he would be in the parking lot and on his way with your valuable merchandise, merchandise that your store had entrusted to you. You began to think that he might get away with the merchandise and the crime. You knew that you had to act and you had to do it quickly.

Your loud voice not only surprised your clerks and others in the front of the store, but surprised even you. You heard yourself yelling for the individual to stop. As you approached the customer, you noticed the perplexed look on his face. He appeared puzzled, perhaps embarrassed, and asked you what you wanted. You asked him to come back to your office to answer some questions. You told him that the store's watch display, which he had been standing near earlier, appeared to be missing several watches and that you were required to question him about the missing watches. He replied that he never took any watches from your store and said you were crazy. He turned to go. You grabbed his arm and told him that under your state's law, you had the power to detain him for questioning since the crime of shoplifting had been committed in your store. You also informed him that you would call the police about the matter and that your store would be pressing charges against him for retail theft. He angrily replied that he never touched the watches on the display rack and that he was no thief. Still holding him by the arm, you escorted him to your office, asked him to sit, and then you called the police, reported the crime, and requested their assistance.

A short while later, two police officers arrived and you told them you believed the individual before them had stolen several watches from the display rack in the store. The customer became belligerent and told the police he did no such thing. He said he was looking at a watch on the display to see what time it was because he had to get back to work. He indicated that he needed to get back to work or he would be late. Ignoring his comments, you handed the police a written statement you had quickly prepared indicating what had happened and further stating that your store wished to prosecute the thief to the full extent of the law. The police took the individual into custody and left. At the police station, the individual was searched, found not to have any watches or other stolen merchandise in his possession, booked into jail based on your signing of the warrant, and then released on his own recognizance since he had been employed for several years at the local ice-packing plant.

A few days later, you were notified by the district attorney's office that it would not pursue the case since there was no evidence that the individual stole anything. Indeed, the prosecutor said that you even noted that you couldn't see his hands during the time he was near the display, that neither you nor your fellow employee actually witnessed the individual taking a watch, and that apparently you had inferred he had taken a watch given his appearance and his position near the display. You told the prosecutor that you were sure he took a watch and proffered that the police might have missed it when they searched him. The prosecutor didn't respond well to your musings and told you not to waste the time of the district attorney's office or the police anymore.

One afternoon some weeks later, a stranger approached you in the store. He inquired as to your name and asked if you were the store's manager. You told him your name and replied that you were the store's manager. He handed you a document and said that he was delivering a summons to you. A summons? As you perused the document, you discovered it indicated that you and the store were being sued. It further indicated that the complaint grew from an incident two months earlier in which an illegal apprehension and false arrest had occurred in your store. The document indicated that the incident had caused substantial embarrassment and public humiliation to the complainant. You recognized the complainant's name as the individual wearing the jacket that you had observed standing near the watch display and for whom you had called the police. The suit asked for the awarding of a significant sum for damages arising from actions you took in apprehending the suspicious-looking individual in your store.

It couldn't be. Surely, the customer wouldn't sue. Surely he understood that you were just doing your job. Surely the law protected you and the store from having to pay damages for your concerned efforts to protect your property rights. Surely the customer couldn't recover any damages; after all, you were only doing your job.

Yeah, right.

SHOPLIFTING BACKGROUND AND PROBLEMS

Shoplifting is the costliest crime impacting retail stores. Extrapolating data estimates included in the "1997 National Retail Security Survey: Final Report" (Hollinger, Dabney, Lee & Hayes, 1997) indicates that over $21 billion worth of merchandise was stolen from domestic retail stores in 1996. Using Survey estimates of losses, one finds that approximately $9.1 billion was taken by outside shoplifters, $10.7 billion was taken by employees of the stores, and another $1.5 billion was stolen by vendor representatives who enter stores ostensibly to conduct business affairs. Regardless of whether the merchandise was stolen by employees, "customers," or vendor representatives, the end result is the same—the crime of shoplifting (retail theft) occurred. The taking of retail merchandise without payment will be referred to throughout this book as shoplifting. The existence of an employment relationship between a retail store and that of a perpetrator of a retail theft, if any, is insignificant. The stealing of retail goods and services is a crime, the crime of theft, the crime of shoplifting. The value of stolen goods and misappropriated services is unfathomably high. The costs associated with the prevention of shoplifting are high, too, as stores seek technologically effective methods of prevention, hire security guards, train their employees to be aware of the problem, and pursue a host of other avenues, all to stem the flow of stolen goods.

To the $21 billion in the direct cost of stolen merchandise or misappropriated services, add the more than $250 million spent by retailers annually in attempts to deter shoplifters and prevent shoplifting, and then the cost of the crime to retail merchants takes on a more egregious magnitude. Indeed, shoplifting is said to be the cause of one-third of all retail bankruptcies. In other words, shoplifters are robbing stores to death, directly causing one-third of all retail bankruptcies. Sadly, no store type seems to be immune from the problem, as implied by the case of a religious bookstore that apprehended ministers who had been pilfering Bibles. Indeed, in this particular case, the ministers who were caught stealing Bibles were street ministers who ostensibly stole Bibles to be in a position to give them to those whom they deemed needed "saving."

Smithsonian magazine (Ryan, 1974) reported that a "school" of shoplifting, which taught the ins and outs of the crime, existed in the 1970s. The idea that an institution that teaches shoplifting to the general public could exist is a sad commentary on modern times. More recently, such "schools" have taken on a modern, high-tech twist. Internet Web sites that provide the same type of information have sprung up. Now, thanks to the information age, factual information, and, it may be argued by some, encouragement are readily available in the privacy of one's own home. Information on how best to commit retail theft is but a phone call away. Individuals desiring to profit from illegal activities such as shoplifting can receive helpful advice via the Internet, ostensibly from individuals making a living shoplifting.

It should be pointed out that several Web sites that provide prevention, deterrence, and legal information surrounding shoplifting have also come online. As such, these provide a service to those trying to minimize the problem's deleterious effects. There are now numerous Web sites providing useful information concerning shoplifting and related laws. Attorneys specializing in shoplifting issues, commercial firms specializing in civil recovery efforts, and a host of other individuals and firms are online and readily available via the Internet. Since the Internet is growing quickly, thousands of sites are added daily, sites are changing, and sites are terminated regularly, a listing of sites at any one time may be fruitless. Accordingly, a listing of Web sites will not be included in this text. However, individuals desiring additional information beyond that available in this book or through the reference section provided at the end of the book are encouraged to search the Web. Search terms that are relevant include shoplifting, civil recovery, shoplifting law, merchant protection statutes, retail theft, and retail civil liability, among others. A search on any of these terms will result in a plethora of sites with relevant information. Then, too, as with any search listing, there will no doubt be sites on the listing that will not prove useful.

In addition to the costs retailers bear directly, society also "pays" for the illegal activities of the thieves. The cost of apprehension, prosecution, and law enforcement associated with the problem is significant. In the United States, approximately 7 million people are caught shoplifting each year, and between 600,000 and 1,000,000 end up being prosecuted. The number of cases is staggering and represent a burden on an already heavily loaded court system. For instance, in at least one jurisdiction, a court was established just to handle the flood of shoplifting cases. In another jurisdiction, a judge estimated that one-third of the cases she tried were shoplifting related. The legal and law enforcement costs of these cases is staggering, and as may be surmised, honest citizens are paying for the law enforcement and judicial costs associated with the crime.

Public tax coffers, as well, take a big hit by shoplifters. Shoplifting results in lost sales, which reduces income for retailers. Lowered income results in retailers paying lower income taxes than they would otherwise have to pay. Estimates of lost income taxes are difficult to make, but conservatively would be several hundred million dollars and possibly could exceed $1 billion. Shoplifting reduces the level of sales taxes by the amount that would be paid on legitimately purchased merchandise, thus negatively impacting local governmental and school coffers to the tune of over $1 billion annually. Shoplifting's negative impact on tax coffers can be seen readily. What is more difficult to see is the direct impact shoplifting has on the typical citizen.

It is estimated that the average family of four spends over $200 annually in the form of higher retail prices, in essence helping to pay for the shoplifting thievery of others. In other words, in setting prices, merchants try to allow for some coverage of their so-called shrinkage (the largest part of which results from shoplifting and employee theft). As one may surmise, though consumers pay for thievery in the form of higher prices, the potential for stores to adequately cover the cost of stolen goods on a parity basis merely by raising prices is unrealistic. Competitive and other market pressures mitigate against stores being able to offset both the total value of lost goods and services and the funds expended to prevent or deter their theft. If stores could simply raise their prices on a parity basis to cover the entirety of their shoplifting costs, it would be an easy problem for stores to handle, though perhaps a bit costly for consumers. Unfortunately, covering the cost of shoplifting is not an easy problem to solve. While store managers may set prices with an eye towards obtaining a certain target return from their offerings, taking account of expected shrinkage in their calculations, they seldom if ever are able to come out on top of the situation by merely raising their prices.

Adding insult to injury is the fact that stores often find themselves the target of lawsuits filed on behalf of customers who feel they have been egregiously harmed by store employees who were taking actions aimed at protecting the property rights of their employers. Legal actions for false arrest, humiliation, illegal apprehension, and similar charges arising from antishoplifting efforts can increase other costs of operating a retail business. Retailers have to cover legal costs associated with these suits, including increased liability insurance premiums, compensation to employees for their time spent in defending against such actions, travel, and a myriad of lesser costs.

In sum, shoplifting is a serious crime that detrimentally impacts retailers of all types. Tens of billions of dollars are lost annually by retailers, government coffers are shortchanged to the tune of billions of dollars, and the continued existence of many stores is imperiled by shoplifters. On top of all of that, store owners and employees are at risk of being sued for pursuing their property rights. The outcome of each suit and amount of damages awarded (if any) varies, depending on the specifics of each case. Damage awards amounting to tens of thousands of dollars are not rare. The recent trend towards suits seeking increasingly larger sums for damages appears unabated. Profitability and store survival are further placed at risk when such suits are won or, as is more often the case, settled out of court.

The problems for retail merchants associated with shoplifting are many. Stores lose sales, have lowered income levels, have higher liability insurance premiums, and are potentially at risk of being sued for efforts associated with shoplifting prevention. The scope of the problem takes on more importance when it is coupled with the question of what to do about shoplifters and their actions. How does one go about detecting and preferably deterring shoplifting?

Much research has been conducted on how best to deal with the problem of shoplifting. Numerous attempts have been made to profile the typical shoplifter. It has been hypothesized that if one could detail a description of the average shoplifter, then one could be on the lookout for that type of person, take appropriate preventive measures, and reduce shoplifting losses. In other words, if the typical shoplifter was a 16-year-old female who wore blue jeans and had her hair tied in a pony tail, then it would be a simple job of being on the lookout for such a female and to follow or observe her during the time she spent in a particular store. Unfortunately, the majority of such research has been inconclusive or, at best, has concluded that the average shoplifter looks no different from other individuals who enter a store. In other words, while some shoplifters may appear nervous, the great majority will dress and look like a store's typical customer or employee. Vigilance by responsible employees on the sales floor is imperative.

Similarly, if the answer to shoplifting was to locate in a particular type of shopping center, like a mall, or in a particular type of neighborhood, then it would again be easy to reduce shoplifting losses. One would have only to locate stores in the "better" neighborhoods or upscale locations to reduce or eliminate shoplifting. At the same time, one would want to avoid locating in the "bad" neighborhoods where shoplifting, ostensibly, would be centered. Unfortunately, such appears not to be the case. According to at least one study, locating in a "good" neighborhood was seen by store manager respondents as being the least viable method mentioned as a way of reducing shoplifting in stores. As one retail store manager whose store was located in an upscale, expensive neighborhood adroitly observed, his location got him a higher class of shoplifter, not fewer shoplifters. And as one would guess, location conceivably would have little or no bearing on the shoplifting activities of employees.

It is difficult for many retail managers to come to grips with the fact that much of the shoplifting in their stores is perpetrated by their own employees. In a survey of store managers by the author, the great majority reported that their employees were not stealing from their stores. But in contrast, discussions with and reports from security personnel paint a different picture of the situation.

For instance, *The Wall Street Journal* reported in 1990 ("Worker Theft," 1990) that a supermarket chain in Los Angeles had fired eighteen employees for shoplifting in one month, compared to a normal employee dismissal rate for that firm of no more than five per year. More recently, a retail security manager of another store chain, while discussing his firm's loss experiences as part of a loss prevention seminar, reported that four of his firm's managers and a district supervisor had been fired after being caught in a theft ring. Retail employees often earn less than employees in the manufacturing sector, and perhaps this increases the likelihood of their stealing from employers. A study by Greenberg (1990) reported that lowered compensation rates were related to employee theft rates. For whatever reason, the incidence of shoplifting is high, and employees are often involved.

As mentioned, numerous studies have attempted to profile the typical shoplifter. Most such studies fail to discern any "type" of shoplifter. In some studies, typical or average shoplifter profiles are noted, but usually such profiles are heavily dependent on the store type and profile of the average shopper patronizing such stores. For instance, a store that caters to teenage females is likely to catch more teenage females shoplifting than middle-aged males. On the other hand, a hardware store that caters to a predominantly male clientele is more likely to catch males stealing than females. Similarly, a store in an area that is predominantly comprised of members of a particular minority is likely to have more thefts committed by members of that minority than by nonminorities.

Income or wealth as a variable for predicting shoplifting proneness has generally failed to distinguish between shoplifters and non-shoplifters. In a similar vein, as previously mentioned, stores that cater to wealthy shoppers are more likely to find a disproportionate share of wealthy shoplifters. Indeed, in one survey of store managers, one manager mentioned that having a location in a good neighborhood resulted in his store catching wealthier shoplifters, not fewer.

Other studies have attempted to understand shoplifting activities of students, to estimate the economic impact of shoplifting, to understand the impact of parental influence on shoplifting behavior of children, and even to examine the relationship of biorhythms to shoplifting behavior. In the biorhythm-shoplifting connection study (Budden, Miller, & Griffin, 1996), the authors investigated whether shoplifting behavior was related to biorythmic criticality. If their investigation had shown that such a relationship existed, new avenues for effective deterrence via employee biorythmic charting and management control logically could have ensued. In other words, had the authors found a relationship between one's biorythmic critical state and proneness to shoplift, employers would only have to produce biorhythm charts for their employees, note which days were critical for each employee, and then provide employment assignments on critical days that minimized opportunities for employees to steal. However, in that investigation, involving over 109,000 shoplifting incidents, the authors noted that no managerially useful relationship between biorhythms and shoplifting proneness was found to exist.

Despite the legal complexities and arguably lengthy prosecutions that shoplifting apprehensions may present to store managements, there is less than adequate attention devoted to the crime in many quarters. Because of this, many stores are stressing shoplifting deterrence as a viable alternative to apprehension. According to *Chain Store Age Executive* (1986), a multifaceted approach in which deterrence plays a central role may provide store managers with a strategy that would likely prove to be an improvement over singular-tactic policies. Still, the potential liability that may arise from a store manager, employee, or other agent of a store pursuing the store's property rights is reason to have knowledge of state statutes that relate to merchant detention efforts and to plan loss control strategies with an understanding of those statutes.

Despite the lack of a definitive shoplifter profile, the increasingly costly nature of the shoplifting problem, and the possibility of being sued for pursuing courses of action to minimize shoplifting losses, all is not hopeless. And in fact, there is some good news. Through effective, organized lobbying by retailers and retail associations, merchants have managed to get state legislatures to pass laws that offer to protect merchants in their efforts to prevent the crime and deter or detain shoplifters. These so-called merchant protection statutes vary in their wording and scope, but in general, they offer merchants a protection privilege that potentially exempts them from paying damages arising from their good faith actions taken in response to incidents in which they have probable cause to believe a shoplifting has occurred.

In addition to these merchant protection statutes, which have been on individual state law books for many years, stores in every state and the District of Columbia have more recently sought and acquired the support of their state legislatures or governing body for pursuing what many merchants had at one time only dreamed of, namely, the ability to file simple civil recovery claims against shoplifters. Civil recovery laws allow retailers to recover monies from shoplifters not just for the value of merchandise that was the object of an attempted theft, but also for help in defraying their prevention costs. Civil recovery laws are seen as significant developments by retailers, who envision making individuals caught shoplifting really "pay" for their crime.

Together, merchant protection statutes and civil recovery laws offer retailers some help in dealing with a problem that continues to escalate. The laws intend to protect merchants from frivolous lawsuits while simultaneously giving them some recompense for their prevention efforts. Still, if stores and their employees are being sued successfully and failing to recover damages, then something must be wrong. Well, it is and it isn't. To take advantage of the legal protection offered by such laws, one needs to know the law and follow its specifics. Failure to know the law and to follow its specifics can result in a store being held accountable, legally, for the actions of its employees and being in a position of being unable to recover for its efforts. To assure a merchant's obtaining the maximum benefits of state law, one needs to develop an effective plan of action aimed at systematically and lawfully approaching the problem.

FORMING A PLAN OF ACTION

In developing a plan of action, retailers should make themselves aware of their state's statutes concerning the apprehension and detention of shoplifting suspects. A retail manager should develop a shoplifting deterrence plan and, just as important, an apprehension policy that would incorporate expectations of state law and meet the letter of state law. This plan of action, which employees of the store would follow in situations where shoplifting is occurring, would best be a written policy detailing how shoplifting incidents would be handled and who would handle them (the employee, security guards, the manager, etc.). The policy should be written in clear, easy-to-understand language and should be specific as to how a shoplifting incident is to be handled. Ideally, there should be little or no room for "creative interpretation" by employees as to how they are to behave before, during, and following the apprehension and detention of a shoplifting suspect. The policy should be specific and emphasize legal concepts. For those situations that will occur that are not covered by the store's policy, common courtesy and a sense of caution should prevail. When people are treated courteously, they are more likely to respond in kind. When people are treated rudely and without regard to their rights, they are likely to feel harmed and pursue courses of action they feel are justified in attempts to punish those who they feel have harmed them.

Make no mistake about it, merchant protection statutes and other shoplifting laws are just that—laws. They cover complex situations, are subject to change over time, and vary in their specifics from one locale to another. It is important—no, imperative—that a retail executive seek competent legal counsel when preparing a store's strategic response to shoplifting. The information contained in this book should not be construed to be legal advice, for it is not. Rather, the information in this book should provide retail managers with knowledge of shoplifting, actions and behaviors that have led to suits, and the results of various cases claiming harm from store employee actions, and thus serve as a basis on which managers can pursue intelligent discussions with their attorneys about how best to protect their stores' property interests.

As a consequence of the central role the law plays in providing merchants protection from damage awards, the next step in the plan would involve an examination of the store's policy statements by competent legal counsel to ensure that its specifics are within the scope of the relevant state statute. Advice from competent legal counsel on the legality, soundness, and completeness of a store's shoplifting policy is necessary to assure that the protection a state's merchant protection statute offers will be there when needed. The importance of having legal counsel in on the plan's evaluation, and even in on its early development, cannot be overemphasized. Merchant protection statutes are laws, and smart executives will acquire competent legal counsel to assist in preparing strategic responses to shoplifting.

In most states, retail store managers and their employees enjoy a so-called conditional privilege, which allows them to apprehend and detain persons suspected of shoplifting from their stores. The conditional privilege of apprehension and detention exists so that store managers or store employees may investigate incidents where grounds exist to believe that a retail theft has occurred. So long as the manager and his or her employees are aware of the law and its specific requirements, understand the law's implications relative to their behaviors, and act in accord with its provisions, the store and its employees should be protected from paying damages as a result of a civil suit arising from the circumstances surrounding an apprehension and detention.

That is why the next step in the plan would require that employees of a store be trained and educated with regard to a written store policy that has been examined and approved by legal counsel. If a store's employees are unaware of the store's policy or the employees fail to follow a legal course of action as detailed in a policy based on the law, the store and its employees will find they are at risk. As will be seen in later chapters, numerous plaintiffs (individuals bringing suit), have prevailed in their civil suits against merchants (the defendants) because employees admitted to not knowing their stores' policies; in some cases, knowing but not following their stores' policies; or, in still other cases, having and following policies that were counter to state law. Training employees to follow a legal course of action is important if the conditional privilege offered by merchant detention statutes and the offer of protection inherent in the statutes are to be realized.

The next step in the plan should involve policy enforcement actions. It is imperative that expectations of employees relative to store policy be enforced. For instance, if a store's policy includes a directive that employees committing retail theft be discharged following an employee discharge process hearing, then following such a hearing, employees shown to have been stealing should be discharged. If a policy statement includes the requirement that the store manager or security guard be alerted immediately when a shoplifter is spotted, then such a course of action should be expected. If a policy spells out the expectation that an employee will continuously observe a shoplifting suspect until an apprehension is attempted, then the expectation that a continuous observation will occur must be clear.

If it is a store's policy, a result of state law, or the result of court rulings pursuant to a case that apprehensions must occur outside of a store proper, then efforts to comply should be expected of employees involved in an apprehension. And surely if store policy dictates restraint and professionalism on the part of store employees, store management should ensure that such occurs. Failure to provide proper training to store employees and failure to enforce store policy can only lead to confusion, low morale, and inefficient efforts to protect the store's property. Worse, and germane to the purposes of this discussion, such failures can lead to the awarding of civil judgments against a store and/or its employees, despite the existence of merchant protection statutes. Enforcing a legal, intelligent antishoplifting policy is a must if one is to gain the benefits of merchant protection statutes and effective store policies.

Essentially, those are the steps in developing an effective plan of action aimed at protecting retailers from shoplifters who sue or from other individuals who might be apprehended or questioned during a potential shoplifting investigation. Develop a written policy that gives specific guidance on how alleged shoplifting incidents are to be handled and details the expectations of all employees concerned. Have the policy examined by competent legal counsel or, better yet, develop it in cooperation with your store's legal counsel, to assure that the policy will meet your store's antishoplifting needs while also meeting legal expectations pursuant to your state's laws. Such a review by your legal counsel is essential, since laws vary among the states and even within a state over time. Educate your employees about the critical role they play in the process and your expectations as to their behavior during a shoplifting incident. Again, be specific about the actions employees are to follow. Be sure to enforce the store's policy as it relates to employee expectations. Making sure your employees are aware of and understand the store's law-based policy and insisting that they follow it are of paramount importance if one is to take maximum advantage of the protection that merchant protection statutes offer stores.

The next chapter gives examples of several states' merchant protection statutes so that the reader may note the types of similarities and differences that exist among the states' statutes. While the ways in which state legislatures have worked to tackle the problem of shoplifting vary, as does the wording of their statutes, their intents are remarkably similar. State merchant protection statutes offer merchants in every state protection from civil suits filed by individuals who feel they have been wronged by merchants. As long as merchants are acting in good faith and according to their state's law, they will be protected. The statutes presented in the next chapter are shown for expository purposes. Throughout this book, the terms "merchant protection statute" and "merchant detention statute" are used interchangeably and refer to the same law. It should be remembered that merchant protection statutes are not some kind of civil cards by which wrongdoers "get out of jail free." Rather, they conditionally offer civil immunity to store managers, their employees, and sometimes others involved in store security when these persons act in good faith and according to the law to protect their property interests.

SUMMARY OF CONCEPTS IN CHAPTER ONE

1. Shoplifting is a crime that negatively impacts retailing.

2. Annually, shoplifting theft in the United States accounts for merchandise losses valued in excess of $21 billion.

3. Hundreds of millions of dollars are spent annually by retail merchants in the attempt to deter or prevent shoplifting.

4. Annually, over $1 billion is lost to state and local tax coffers due to the reduction of retail sales resulting from shoplifting and the corresponding decrease in the amount of sales taxes collected.

5. The cost associated with the impact of shoplifting on the justice system is high.

6. Shoplifting is attributable to the criminal actions of employees, nonemployee customers, and vendor representatives.

7. No type of retail store is immune from the shoplifting problem.

8. Merchants should develop an effective, lawful plan of action with which to deal with the problem of shoplifting. Employees should be trained to follow the plan.

9. Merchants are granted conditional immunity from civil liability when they take lawful actions to deter shoplifting.

10. States have enacted merchant civil recovery laws, with the result that stores can get recompense for some of the costs associated with the shoplifting problem.

Chapter Two

Merchant Protection Statutes

Shoplifting, the taking of retail merchandise without proper payment, is a crime. It is a crime that wreaks havoc on the profitability and survivability of retail stores. It matters little whether the individual taking the merchandise without proper payment is an employee of the store or is not an employee of the store. The taking of retail merchandise without proper payment is referred to as shoplifting. Shoplifting is a criminal offense in every state, and as such, carries criminal penalties. Since shoplifting statutes are state laws, they vary in their wording, in their impact, in the protection they afford merchants and others who have to deal with persons whom they have cause to believe were stealing their goods or services, and in their expectations of the efforts that retailers may take in pursuing their property rights.

Some states' legislatures have enacted, as has Pennsylvania's, statutes that define and deal specifically with shoplifting. Many states though, handle the problem as does the state of Louisiana, which deals with shoplifting under general theft statutes. And still other states have laws governing shoplifting and related acts similar to California's statute dealing with the theft of retail merchandise, library books, and the illegal recording of motion pictures by theater patrons, or Florida's statute, which deals with retail theft and efforts associated with the apprehension of individuals stealing farm produce. Retail executives and others involved in retail security tend to agree that specific shoplifting laws are better suited to handle such matters than are general theft statutes. Regardless of the jurisdiction in which the crime is committed or how the theft is prosecuted, shoplifting is a crime and carries with it criminal penalties in every state.

Shoplifting statutes and their merchant protection stipulations are very specific as to the rights and responsibilities of retail merchants and their employees and/or agents in dealing with the problem of shoplifting. Again, these rights and responsibilities vary among the states and sometimes among the classes of individuals involved (e.g., store employees or security guards), but the more common factors include the following.

1. Most states' statutes empower merchants to detain suspects for questioning or investigating circumstances surrounding a potential intent to steal merchandise. More often than not, these statutes do not empower the merchant to "arrest" suspects but merely to detain them for investigation purposes or to facilitate the arrest of the individual by law enforcement officers. The detention must be lawful. It must be based on a strong belief that a retail theft has occurred or is in the process of occurring. Retail merchants have a "conditional privilege" of apprehension and detention. The condition is that to effect an apprehension, a merchant must harbor more than mere suspicion. The privilege does not allow merchants the right to stop and question every suspicious-looking person who enters a store. The merchant must believe, and have a strong reason to believe, that a theft is occurring before initiating an apprehension. As will be seen in several of the cases to be mentioned, merchants find themselves vulnerable to suits alleging damages when it is revealed that apprehensions and detentions are not based on a reasonable belief that a crime has occurred, but rather are the result of some other factor (e.g., the person appears to be suspicious). The possession of a strong, reasonable belief that a theft has occurred, sometimes referred to as possessing reasonable or probable cause, should stand at the heart of all apprehensions.

2. As might be guessed, no state or jurisdiction empowers merchants to use deadly force in apprehending and detaining shoplifting suspects, although most relevant statutes do allow merchants to use "reasonable force" in apprehending and detaining suspected shoplifters. Reasonable force is just that, reasonable. It does not usually involve threats of bodily harm; nor does it normally involve unilateral physical actions that could be considered offensive in nature. At the same time, reasonableness varies according to the circumstances of the apprehension and the response of individuals apprehended. Some circumstances will require more intervention on the part of the store employee than will others. Again, security personnel recognize that the world is becoming an increasingly dangerous place in which to conduct a retail business. Still, most incidents of retail theft or shoplifting are not violent in nature, and store employees must recognize such. Reasonable force does not equate with excessive use of force, and store employees must act prudently.

3. Merchants can detain suspects only for a reasonable length of time or for the maximum amount of time specified by a particular state's law.

Merchant protection statutes allow merchants the right to apprehend and detain shoplifting suspects for the purpose of investigating a probable retail theft. Such investigations should be specific, complete, and relatively quick. When it is apparent that an arrest will follow such an apprehension, police need to be summoned quickly, charges pressed, and the individual handed over to the police. The concept that an apprehension and detention be of a reasonable duration is to ensure that innocent individuals are inconvenienced as little as possible. Reasonableness varies according to the circumstances, but store employees are advised not to take an undue amount of time to investigate shoplifting incidents. Some states' statutes, as does Louisiana's, specify that detentions be for no more than one hour. Obviously, one would want to assure that any apprehension in Louisiana or other jurisdictions that limit the time to one hour are concluded within one hour. To do otherwise is to expose one's store and oneself to civil liability. Further discussion and considerations regarding the length of legal detentions are discussed in Chapter 5.

4. While some states do allow cursory searching of suspects, especially as it involves such items as handbags, shopping bags, baby buggies, and other items in the possession of shoplifting suspects, statutes generally do not provide merchants the right to search inside a suspect's clothing, and as will be seen later, no state statute bestows on store employees the right to strip search suspects. Indeed, many would be surprised at the number and types of incidences in which allegations of undressing or some form of clothing removal by store employees is alleged. Allegations of this type are seen in some of the cases discussed in Chapter 4. Restrictions on the part of store employees as to bodily searches should not deter store employees from pursuing their stores' property rights. Individuals who are arrested by police will be subject to a search by law enforcement officers before being jailed. The employee should report to the arresting officers what items were stolen and where the suspect was seen hiding them on his or her person. For a store employee to do otherwise, that is, to conduct a search inside a suspect's clothing or to require that a suspect disrobe to prove his or her innocence, places the store employee and the store at great risk.

Merchant protection statutes typically protect retail merchants and their employees from paying damages alleged to have been incurred through suits filed by persons apprehended for shoplifting in cases where merchants and/or their employees acted in good faith to protect their business and property interests. These statutes generally allow merchants to use reasonable force in apprehending and detaining persons suspected of shoplifting. The statutes incorporate a maximum length of time a shoplifting suspect may be detained or allow detentions for reasonable lengths of time so as to allow the merchant time to investigate and, if needed, time to allow the merchant the opportunity to request law enforcement assistance. Ostensibly, the maximum length of time an individual is allowed to be detained is stipulated to prevent merchants from intruding on the rights of law-abiding citizens.

The relevant statutes of Florida, California, Kansas, Kentucky, and Michigan are included in this chapter for expository purposes and to emphasize that differences and similarities do exist between the various states' statutes. Alabama's merchant detention statute will serve as the basis for further discussion. Again, it should be pointed out that each state's law varies, and over time, a particular state's law may change, so it is recommended that store managers seek the advice of their legal counsel when preparing shoplifting control strategies, to insure that specific efforts are deemed reasonable and legal as it pertains to the state in which a manager operates.

Alabama's Law on Shoplifting (AL ST § 15-10-14)

(a) A peace officer, a merchant or a merchant's employee who has probable cause for believing that goods held for sale by the merchant have been unlawfully taken by a person and that he can recover them by taking the person into custody may, for the purpose of attempting to effect such recovery, take the person into custody and detain him in a reasonable manner for a reasonable length of time. Such taking into custody and detention by a peace officer, merchant or merchant's employee shall not render such police officer, merchant or merchant's employee criminally or civilly liable for false arrest, false imprisonment or unlawful detention.

(b) Any peace officer may arrest without warrant any person he has probable cause for believing has committed larceny in retail or wholesale establishments.

(c) A merchant or a merchant's employee who causes such arrest as provided for in subsection (a) of this section of a person for larceny of goods held for sale shall not be criminally or civilly liable for false arrest or false imprisonment where the merchant or merchant's employee has probable cause for believing that the person arrested committed larceny of goods held for sale.

While the next three chapters will detail experiences specific store managers encountered in trying to deal with the problem of shoplifting, a small explanation of each of these three sections is called for here. Each section has implications for retail strategy development.

First, section (a) of the Alabama statute is explicit about who is protected under the statute. As seen in the statute, the Alabama legislature saw fit to extend protection to law enforcement officers, store owners, and store employees. Alabama extends a conditional privilege of apprehension and detention to these three groups, only. Many states' statutes are similar, but as will be seen, some states' statutes extend protection to third party security guards and other agents, who are not normally considered employees of stores but instead are working under contract to stores. While the absence of civil protection for third party security guards will probably not be of concern to store managers, since store managers are offered protection, it will be of specific importance to those operating security services for retailers because they may be exposed to situations where they risk liability exposure.

Alabama law is not unusual in specifying that a detention be conducted in a reasonable manner. This places the burden on the store manager to assure that reasonable measures are implemented in handling shoplifting incidents. Assaulting shoplifting suspects is not likely to be deemed reasonable anywhere, but given the increased level of violence in the workplace, the use of a reasonable level of self-defense may sometimes be necessary. At the same time, experienced store security personnel will be among the first to recommend against taking unnecessary risks with potentially violent shoplifters. A security manager for a department store in Louisiana, in describing a particular incident to the author, said the shoplifter pulled out a knife and, threatening, pointed it towards her, whereupon she jumped back and told him to go ahead and take the merchandise. Wisely, she figured it was a much better idea to describe the shoplifter and his vehicle to the police than to risk being seriously injured or killed for an item of store merchandise. Prudence during the apprehension of shoplifting suspects who potentially could cause harm to employees is always a wise course of action. The author agrees with the security manager, who stated her belief that no piece of store merchandise is worth the price of a serious injury or, worse, a death.

Merchants and their employees, while offered the privilege of apprehending and detaining individuals suspected of shoplifting, are limited by statute as to the length of time during which a detention for shoplifting investigation may be conducted. Alabama law is not unusual in specifying that a detention not be for more than a "reasonable length of time." Indeed, most states' merchant protection statutes offer their protection from civil liability when detentions and subsequent investigations are deemed to be for a reasonable length of time. A few states' statutes approach the duration of a legal merchant detention in a specific manner, as does Louisiana's, which allows merchants to detain shoplifting suspects for sixty minutes (one hour). Incorporating a sixty-minute time limit in a state statute ostensibly grows from the belief of some legislatures that one hour is a reasonable length of time for a store employee to investigate an incident, summon police, and allow time for the police to arrive and make an arrest. Still, regardless of the length of time allowed by state law, it should be noted that time limits are stated so as to minimize intrusions on law-abiding citizens. So, even disregarding Louisiana's statute allowing a store employee one hour to investigate a probable theft, prudence would dictate that the employee investigate such matters in a timely manner.

The remainder of this chapter displays the merchant protection statutes of selected states for comparison purposes. Including every states' statute in this discourse would not add to the understanding of the problem but would only serve to add "bulk" to this discussion. Each retail executive should obtain a copy of his or her state's statute regarding merchant detention, discuss it with legal counsel, and include its specifics in shoplifting policy statements.

Chapter 3 will discuss the concept of identifying suspects and a closely related concept, the concept of having probable cause. Lacking cause, a store owner or an employee of a store does not enjoy the conditional privilege of apprehension and detention allowed under state statute. More important, the protection from paying damages arising from suits related to shoplifting apprehensions will not accrue to individuals who lack probable cause. It is for this reason that the next chapter's focus, that of establishing cause in the identification of a suspect, is central to the remainder of this book. Possessing probable cause before pursuing an apprehension and detention is of paramount importance if store owners are to enjoy the protection that merchant protection statutes offer.

Examples of Merchant Protection Statutes

[Florida Statutes § 812.-015 (3)]: (a) A law enforcement officer, a merchant, a merchant's employee, or a farmer who has probable cause to believe that retail or farm theft has been committed by a person and that he can recover the property by taking the person into custody may, for the purpose of attempting to effect such recovery or for prosecution, take the person into custody and detain him in a reasonable manner for a reasonable length of time. In the case of a farmer, taking into custody shall be effectuated only on property owned or leased by the farmer. In the event the merchant, merchant's employee or farmer takes the person into custody, a law enforcement officer shall be called to the scene immediately after the person has been taken into custody. (5) A merchant, merchant's employee, or farmer who takes a person into custody, as provided in subsection (3), or who causes an arrest, as provided in subsection (4), of a person for retail theft or farm theft shall not be criminally or civilly liable for false arrest or false imprisonment when the merchant, merchant's employee, or farmer has probable cause to believe that the person committed retail theft or farm theft.

[Kentucky Revised Statutes § 433.236(1)]: (1) A peace officer, security agent of a mercantile establishment, merchant or merchant's employee who has probable cause for believing that goods held for sale by the merchant have been unlawfully taken by a person may take the person into custody and detain him in a reasonable manner for a reasonable length of time, on the premises of the mercantile establishment or off the premises of the mercantile establishment, if the persons enumerated in this section are in fresh pursuit, for any or all of the following purposes: (a) To request identification; (b) to verify such identification; (c) to make reasonable inquiry as to whether such person has in his possession unpurchased merchandise and to make reasonable investigation of the ownership of such merchandise; (d) to recover or attempt to recover goods taken from the mercantile establishment by such person, or by others accompanying him; (e) to inform a peace officer or law enforcement agency of the detention of the person and to surrender the person to the custody of a peace officer.

[California Penal Code § 490.5]: (f) (1) A merchant may detain a person for a reasonable time for the purpose of conducting an investigation in a reasonable manner whenever the merchant has probable cause to believe the person to be detained is attempting to unlawfully take or has unlawfully taken merchandise from the merchant's premises. A theater owner may detain a person for a reasonable time for the purpose of conducting an investigation in a reasonable manner whenever the theater owner has probable cause to believe the person to be detained is attempting to operate a video recording device within the premises of a motion picture theater without the authority of the owner of the theater. A person employed by a library facility may detain a person for a reasonable time for the purpose of conducting an investigation in a reasonable manner whenever the person employed by the library facility has probable cause to believe the person to be detained is attempting to unlawfully remove or has unlawfully removed books or library materials from the premises of the library facility.

(2) In making the detention a merchant, theater owner, or a person employed by a library facility may use a reasonable amount of nondeadly force necessary to protect himself or herself and to prevent escape of the person detained or the loss of tangible or intangible property.

(3) During the period of detention any items which a merchant or theater owner, or any items which a person employed by a library facility has probable cause to believe are unlawfully taken from the premises of the merchant or library facility, or recorded on theater premises, and which are in plain view may be examined by the merchant, theater owner, or person employed by a library facility for the purposes of ascertaining the ownership thereof.

(4) A merchant, theater owner, a person employed by a library facility, or an agent thereof, having probable cause to believe the person detained was attempting to unlawfully take or has taken any item from the premises, or was attempting to operate a video recording device within the premises of a motion picture theater without the authority of the owner of the theater, may request the person detained to voluntarily surrender the item or recording. Should the person detained refuse to surrender the recording or item of which there is probable cause to believe has been recorded on or unlawfully taken from the premises, or attempted to be recorded or unlawfully taken from the premises, a limited and reasonable search may be conducted by those authorized to make the detention in order to recover the item. Only packages, shopping bags, handbags, and other property in the immediate possession of the person detained, but not including any clothing worn by the person, may be searched pursuant to this subdivision. Upon surrender or discovery of the item, the person detained may also be requested, but may not be required, to provide adequate proof of his or her true identity.

(5) If any person admitted to a theater . . . [this paragraph omitted by author since it refers only to illegal recordings in theaters]

(6) a peace officer who accepts custody of a person arrested for an offense contained in this section may, subsequent to the arrest, search the person arrested and his or her immediate possessions for any item or items alleged to have been taken.

(7) In any civil action brought by any person resulting from a detention or arrest by a merchant, it shall be a defense to such action that the merchant detaining or arresting such person had probable cause to believe that the person had stolen or attempted to steal merchandise and that the merchant acted reasonably under all the circumstances.

In any civil action brought by any person resulting from a detention or arrest by a theater owner or person employed by a library facility, it shall be a defense to that action that the theater owner or person employed by a library facility detaining or arresting that person had probable cause to believe that the person was attempting to operate a video recording device within the premises of a motion picture theater without the authority of the owner of the theater or had stolen or attempted to steal books or library materials and that the person employed by a library facility acted reasonably under all the circumstances.

(g) As used in this section: (1) "Merchandise" means any personal property, capable of manual delivery, displayed, held or offered for retail sale by a merchant. (2) "Merchant" means an owner or operator, and the agent, consignee, employee, lessee, or officer of an owner or operator, of any premises used for the retail purchase or sale of any personal property capable of manual delivery. (3) "Theater owner" means an owner or operator, and the agent, employee, consignee, lessee or officer of an owner or operator, of any premises used for the exhibition or performance of motion pictures to the general public. (4) The terms "book or other library materials" include any book, plate, picture, photograph, engraving, painting, drawing, map, newspaper, magazine, pamphlet, broadside, manuscript, document, letter, public record, microform, sound recording, audiovisual material in any format, magnetic or other tape, electronic data-processing record, artifact, or other documentary, written or printed material regardless of physical form or characteristics, or any part thereof, belonging to, on loan to, or otherwise in the custody of a library facility. (5) The term "library facility" includes any public library; any library of an educational, historical, or eleemosynary institution, organization or society; any museum, any repository of public records.

[Kansas Statutes Annotated § 21-3424]: Any merchant, or a merchant's agent or employee, who has probable cause to believe that a person has actual possession of and has wrongfully taken, or is about to wrongfully take merchandise from a mercantile establishment, may detain such person on the premises or in the immediate vicinity thereof, in a reasonable manner and for a reasonable period of time for the purpose of investigating the circumstances of such possession. Such reasonable detention shall not constitute an arrest nor criminal restraint.

[Michigan Compiled Laws Annotated § 600.2917]: (1) In a civil action against a library or merchant, an agent of the library or merchant, or an independent contractor providing security for the library or merchant for false imprisonment, unlawful arrest, assault, battery, libel, or slander, if the claim arises out of conduct involving a person suspected of removing or of attempting to remove, without right or permission, goods held for sales in a store from the store or library materials from a library, or of violating section 356c or 356d of the Michigan penal code, Act No. 328 of the Public Acts of 1931, being sections 750.356c and 750.356d of the Michigan Compiled Laws, and if the merchant, library, agent, or independent contractor had probable cause for believing and did believe that the plaintiff had committed or aided or abetted in the larceny of goods held for sale in the store, or of library materials, or in the violation of section 356c of Act No. 328 of the Public Acts of 1931, damages for or resulting from mental anguish, or punitive, exemplary, or aggravated damages shall not be allowed a plaintiff, unless it is proved that the merchant, library, agent, or independent contractor used unreasonable force, detained the plaintiff an unreasonable length of time, acted with unreasonable disregard of the plaintiff's rights or sensibilities, or acted with intent to injure the plaintiff.

(2) As used in this section: (a) "Library" includes a public library; a library of an educational, historical, or eleemosynary institution or organization; a museum; an archive; and a repository of public records or historical records, or both. (b) "Library material" includes a plate; picture; photograph; engraving; painting; drawing; map; newspaper; book; magazine; pamphlet; broadside; manuscript; document; letter; public record; microfilm; sound recording; audiovisual material; magnetic or other tape; optical storage disc or other recording medium; electronic data processing record; artifact; and other documentary, written, or printed material.

SUMMARY OF CONCEPTS IN CHAPTER TWO

1. Merchant protection (detention) statutes grant merchants a conditional privilege to apprehend and detain persons suspected of shoplifting.

2. The offer of civil liability immunity is conditioned on the merchant having sufficient cause (probable cause) to believe a theft is occurring or has occurred.

3. Merchant detention statutes allow reasonable force to be used to detain individuals suspected of shoplifting.

4. Detentions must be reasonable as to their duration.

5. Investigations conducted pursuant to a detention must be conducted in a reasonable manner.

6. Statutes do not empower merchants to disrobe shoplifting suspects or to order the disrobing of such suspects.

7. Retailers are offered immunity from civil liability when they act lawfully to protect their property.

8. Every state has a merchant protection statute. Such statutes are state laws, and while there are many similarities among the states' statutes, there are some distinct differences. Merchants should know and understand their state's merchant detention statute.

Chapter Three

Identifying a Suspect
(Establishing Cause)

As was seen in the last chapter, merchant protection statutes generally have three primary areas of concern to which attention must be paid in order to take advantage of the protection offered by the statutes. A merchant desiring to take advantage of the conditional privilege offered by merchant protection statutes and enjoy the protection offered as it relates to immunity from paying civil damages must identify a shoplifter, in the sense that the merchant must have adequate cause to believe an individual has shoplifted merchandise from a store. Next, a merchant or store employee must apprehend and detain a suspect in a lawful manner. And finally, the length of time the investigation and detention takes must be legal.

The first area of concern and the one that concerns this chapter is the idea of identifying a shoplifter or, in other words, establishing cause to indicate that an individual is shoplifting. The placement of this concern before the other two does not grow from a chance placement effort. Rightfully, it precedes the other two concerns. If one does not have adequate cause to believe an individual has committed a shoplifting act, then questions surrounding the other two statute concerns should never arise. If one does not have cause to believe an individual has shoplifted merchandise from one's store, then apprehension and detention should not ensue. Without adequate cause to apprehend and detain an individual, any arguments about the lawfulness of a detention or the adherence to reasonable time limits during an investigation are moot.

One must have probable cause to believe a shoplifting incident has occurred before any apprehension is undertaken. One must have probable cause to believe a shoplifting incident has occurred before any detention is undertaken. The existence and possession of adequate probable cause is at the heart of the matter, and without it, merchants may find they are vulnerable to civil suits despite the existence of merchant protection statutes. So, is it not an easy matter to establish adequate probable cause? Can a gut feeling that something is wrong suffice? Can a suspicious-looking individual be apprehended, detained for a period of time, and interrogated because one feels that the individual is perhaps up to no good? What is probable cause and how do merchants know when they have it?

Merchant protection statutes are careful to point out that only those individuals suspected of shoplifting can be legally apprehended and detained. If such a suspicion does not exist or ceases to exist, then the conditional privilege of apprehension and detention does not exist or ceases to exist. The experience of a New Orleans grocery store chain demonstrates one perspective of this concern.

In *Johnson v. Schwegmann Brothers, Inc.*, the store initially possessed the right to detain the suspect but lost it. According to the record, Johnson went to the store to purchase a 69 cent bag of ice. While waiting in the checkout line, he noticed the cashier was waiting for approval of a check given to her by the customer ahead of him. Johnson asked the cashier to accept one dollar as payment for the ice in order that he might leave. She agreed and accepted the dollar. He walked around the customer and went out of the store. In the parking lot, defendant's security guards stopped him to ask for proof of purchase. Since Johnson did not have a receipt, he volunteered to return to the cashier to have his purchase verified. Once in the store, the cashier confirmed Johnson's story.

Thereafter, Johnson and his witnesses told a different story from that of the store's employees as to what happened. Johnson claimed he was forcibly detained in defendant's security office and interrogated. Store employees, on the other hand, claimed that the plaintiff became abusive, threatened to sue, and insisted on being taken to the manager to complain. The trial judge, as trier of fact, believed the plaintiff and awarded damages. The store appealed the decision. The appellate court affirmed the lower court's finding for Johnson and the awarding of damages. The appellate court noted that until the cashier confirmed the payment by the plaintiff, defendant's employees were acting within the conditional privilege granted by Louisiana's merchant detention law. However, once the cashier established that no theft had occurred, immunity from civil liability ceased to exist.

In *Johnson*, initially the store employees had adequate cause to believe the individual had taken the ice without payment, and they then acted lawfully. Upon being asked, Johnson admitted he did not have a receipt and voluntarily returned to the cashier to have his story confirmed. From an outsider's point of view, seldom, if ever, does a store's cashier allow someone to walk out of a store without being checked out. The plaintiff's bypassing the line and his inability to produce a receipt would generate sufficient concern in most stores to initiate an investigation. As such, the initial efforts to confirm payment were within state statute expectations, were privileged, and would have incurred civil immunity protection. Once the cashier confirmed payment, the existence of any cause to believe Johnson had stolen the ice ceased to exist. When the cashier confirmed that Johnson had paid for the ice, Johnson should have been thanked for his help in resolving the matter and immediately released.

A finding similar to that described in Johnson was seen in the case of *Hardin v. Barker's of Monroe, Inc.* In *Hardin*, testimony indicated that Hardin had entered Barker's shoe store with his children. A store security guard testified that he observed Hardin remove price tags from cowboy boots and put them on his two sons. The guard reported seeing Hardin place a pair of shoes in his pocket and, without his children, leave the store. The guard approached Hardin in the parking lot and asked about the shoes in his pocket. Hardin removed the shoes from his pockets. The shoes were old and obviously worn. The guard had Hardin return to the store and escorted him to the office.

Once in the office, Hardin refused to have his pockets searched further. Purportedly, Hardin was thrown to the floor and handcuffed. A search of his pockets turned up only his wallet, which ostensibly contained more money than would be needed to buy several pairs of shoes. Hardin told the guard that the money was to buy his children new shoes. The children were brought into the office but not questioned. Police were called and charges preferred against Hardin. The children reportedly accompanied their father to the police station, where they were retrieved by their mother. Hardin spent two days in jail before posting bond. At his criminal trial on the shoplifting charge, Hardin was acquitted.

After his acquittal, Hardin filed suit against Barker's, claiming damages related to his detention and arrest. The district court entered a judgment in favor of the store. Louisiana's merchant detention statute figured prominently in the deliberations. Louisiana law, as does the law of other states, allows a merchant to use reasonable force to detain an individual when the merchant possesses reasonable cause to believe a crime has been committed. Given that probable or reasonable cause is shown to exist, immunity from civil liability will follow. Hardin appealed, claiming that the store did not possess reason to believe he had committed a crime.

The Court of Appeals of Louisiana, Second Circuit, noted that the store guard initially had reason to believe a crime was being committed. The guard saw Hardin place a pair of shoes in his pocket. The guard saw Hardin leave the store without paying for the shoes. The guard was acting in a privileged manner in his approaching Hardin and asking about the shoes. However, after seeing that the shoes were not store merchandise (they were old shoes) and hearing Hardin's explanation, the guard had a reasonable explanation for the actions he had observed. At that point, probable cause to believe Hardin was committing a crime ceased to exist.

Lacking cause, the guard should have immediately released Hardin. Instead, he escorted him back into the store, reportedly subdued and searched him, and initiated a prosecution. Immunity from civil liability ceased to exist when the probable cause ceased to exist. The actions that followed the initial investigation were not privileged. The appellate court noted that the lower court erred in finding for the store. The judgment in favor of the store was reversed and a monetary judgment was entered in favor of Hardin.

The lack of probable cause, or reasonable cause to detain, results in the elimination of the civil liability immunity offered by merchant detention statutes. If probable cause exists at a point in time but then ceases to exist, the immunity from civil liability that existed ceases to exist. Store employees must have reason to proceed in their efforts against individuals. Lacking such reason, stores will find they are vulnerable to civil damage awards.

In another case, in which a store was found not to be negligent in its handling of an incident, the plaintiff was unable to show that she had been falsely imprisoned or slandered. In *Shaw v. Rose's Stores, Inc. and R. M. Faw*, the plaintiff was seen leaving the store with a sweater tied around her shoulders. A cashier who witnessed Shaw leaving the store noticed that the sweater had a tag on it and alerted the assistant store manager (Faw). Faw went after the plaintiff, and after catching up to her, requested that she accompany him to the cashier so that he could inspect the sweater. She agreed to the request. Once in the store, Faw inspected the sweater and noted that the sweater had not come from Rose's. Indeed, the plaintiff had purchased the sweater from another store more than one month prior to her visit to Rose's. Apparently, the plaintiff had inadvertently left the tag on the sweater. Faw pointed out to the plaintiff that the size tag was still attached with wires to the sweater. He explained that the presence of the tag hanging from the sweater as Shaw exited the store was the basis for their actions. Faw removed the tag, apologized to the plaintiff, and returned the sweater.

The appellate court in North Carolina affirmed the trial court's ruling that the store's employees acted in accordance with North Carolina's merchant detention statute. In this case, there was nothing to indicate that the plaintiff had been unlawfully apprehended or detained. Indeed, the court ruled that the plaintiff failed to show she was illegally detained at all. It noted that she freely and voluntarily went back into the store and received an explanation as to why the cashier assumed she had taken some of the store's merchandise. The appellate court said the plaintiff knew at all times she had not taken any merchandise from the store wrongfully, and as a consequence, the plaintiff had nothing to fear.

Every merchant detention statute is explicit when concerning who may be apprehended and detained. Only those individuals suspected of shoplifting may be legally apprehended and detained. If such a suspicion does not exist or ceases to exist, then the conditional privilege of apprehension and detention does not exist or ceases to exist. Store managers and employees need to be sure that there is sufficient reason to suspect an individual has stolen or is in the process of stealing merchandise from the store before taking overt steps to correct the situation.

The case of *Robinson v. Wieboldt Stores, Inc.* illustrates another incident where probable cause to investigate may have been present initially, but once probable cause ceased to exist, the investigation should have concluded. Robinson purchased a scarf on the first floor of defendant's store. She paid for the purchase with a credit card. After purchasing the scarf, she removed the price tag and handed it to the clerk before placing the scarf around her neck. The clerk gave Robinson the receipt, which she placed in her pocket. The customer then proceeded to the third floor of the store.

Purportedly, as she stepped off the escalator, a security guard grabbed Robinson by the left arm near to her shoulder. He displayed a badge and gave Robinson his name. He proceeded to question her about the scarf and took her to a room. She explained she had purchased the scarf on the first floor and produced the receipt, which the guard took. He continued to hold her by the arm. He then escorted Robinson to the first floor, where the clerk confirmed Robinson had just purchased the scarf. Reportedly, the guard told the sales clerk that she had caused Robinson a lot of trouble. He then walked away without apologizing.

Robinson was very upset by the incident. She immediately went out of the store and vomited. A cab was called, and Robinson went home. She sent a letter to the store manager complaining of the incident, but received no reply. Subsequently, she filed suit for damages for pain and suffering arising from false imprisonment. In addition to compensatory damages, the jury awarded Robinson punitive damages.

The appellate court in its review cited Illinois's merchant detention statute, which provides, in part, that a merchant who has reasonable grounds to believe a person has committed retail theft may detain that person in a reasonable manner and for a reasonable time in order to request identification and verify it, to investigate the ownership of merchandise in the possession of the person, and to inform a police officer of the detention. After reviewing the case, the court concluded that Robinson had been the victim of a false imprisonment. It noted that even after presenting the guard with the sales receipt, the guard required her to go to the first floor of the store.

The appellate court ruled that the issue of whether the guard's actions were reasonable was a factual issue, and rightfully an issue for the jury to decide. The appellate court also upheld the awarding of punitive damages, because it viewed the guard's grabbing of Robinson by the arm, continuing to hold Robinson by the arm after she produced the sales receipt, and taking her to the first floor as a basis for an instruction on punitive damages. The court noted that even though punitive damages are not usually awarded against a corporate defendant for acts committed by an employee, exceptions are made when the principal or managerial agent of the corporation ratifies the act of its employee. The court noted that Wieboldt continued to defend the actions of its guard and showed no attempt to alter its procedures relative to such situations. The court noted that Wieboldt had never apologized to Robinson.

It should be noted that the court, after affirming the jury finding for Robinson in her suit for false imprisonment and request for punitive damages, reversed the specific monetary awards due to what it saw as incompetent medical testimony by Robinson as to her condition. Apparently, the court felt that the lack of expert medical testimony mandated a review of the actual awards. Still, its affirmation that the guard's actions resulted in Robinson being falsely imprisoned should serve as an excellent example of what retailers should strive to avoid in preparing store policy statements. Further, the testimony indicating that the store had not replied to Robinson's letter nor apologized to her emphasizes the necessity for maintaining professionalism and simple courtesy during such incidents.

In a case that ultimately was decided by the Supreme Court of Virginia, the plaintiff's charges arose from an incident in which a store employee accused the plaintiff of willfully concealing merchandise with the intent of stealing the merchandise. In the case of *Tweedy v. J. C. Penney Company, Inc.*, the plaintiff was detained by store employees until police arrived. The police then took her into custody and booked her under the state's larceny statute. Specifically, the state statute specifies that "the willful concealment of goods or merchandise of any store or other mercantile establishment, while still on the premises thereof, shall be prima facie evidence of an intent to commit and defraud the owner out of the value of the goods."

Both parties described similar events leading up to the detention. The plaintiff had entered the store and proceeded to look at slacks.

Tweedy took three pairs of slacks into a dressing room that had a draw curtain for an entrance door. She began trying on the slacks.

This is where the parties began to disagree as to the events that followed. The plaintiff claimed that the first pair did not fit her and that she dropped it over her purse, which lay on the floor of the dressing room. She then began to try on a second pair. The plaintiff said a store employee peeked around the curtain and asked if everything was okay. She responded that everything was fine. The plaintiff claims the employee then reached around her and retrieved the pair of slacks on the floor. Moments later, the employee informed the plaintiff the manager desired to talk to her about her having the "pants in her pocketbook."

The store employee's version of the incident differed in that the employee claimed she saw the plaintiff leaning over her purse, which contained the slacks. She reported that the slacks were rolled tightly and that they were situated completely inside the purse. The employee accused the plaintiff of attempting to steal the slacks and summoned the manager.

The plaintiff was booked and later tried in the General District Court. Her case was dismissed. Following the criminal proceedings, and ostensibly as a consequence of the store employee's actions, the plaintiff filed suit seeking damages for the employee's comments during the incident, which the plaintiff claimed were insulting, and for the store's pursuit of a course of action charged by the plaintiff as a malicious prosecution. In the end, the suit sought only compensatory damages for the plaintiff. Punitive damages, often sought in cases alleging malicious prosecution, were not sought in this case.

The circuit court jury found in favor of the plaintiff. However, the judgment was vacated, the judge ruling that the plaintiff had failed to establish the existence of malice on the part of the store employees. Failure to establish malice on the part of the employees was seen by the judge as necessary for the charges to stand. However, the Supreme Court of Virginia ultimately decided the case in favor of the plaintiff. The supreme court noted that the plaintiff was not required to prove malice in a case seeking compensatory damages for insulting words or malicious prosecution. Malice would have to be shown to have been present only if punitive damages had been sought by the plaintiff. Since there was no attempt to seek punitive damages for the store employees' actions, the finding by the jury for the plaintiff was reinstated.

A man who apparently bought a hat from a discount store and returned a month later wearing it was stopped, arrested, and tried for stealing it. The case of *Gibson Discount Center, Inc. v. Cruz* evolved out of an incident in which Cruz was accused of stealing the hat. Cruz, a city maintenance supervisor, had been shopping with his mother and sister at Gibson's. He reported that he entered the store wearing a hat that he had purchased previously at Gibson's. As he exited the store, Cruz was approached by a security guard, who asked if he had forgotten to pay for anything. Cruz was directed to return to the store and escorted to the back.

Once there, Cruz was questioned about the hat. He replied that he had purchased it some weeks earlier. His mother and sister corroborated his statements to the store employees. After questioning Cruz and listening to his family members, the police were called and charges preferred against Cruz. He was taken to jail, where he spent the night before posting bond and being released.

At his criminal trial, Cruz produced a cash register receipt from Gibson's dated about a month prior to his apprehension. Among the items listed on the tape was a hat. Cruz testified that the hat on the tape was that which he was accused of stealing. Further, he testified that the hat had been soiled from his having worn it for some time and that its condition alone should have indicated that it was not a new hat. Cruz was found innocent of stealing the hat by a jury.

At his civil trial against the store, Cruz again submitted the tape as a component of his evidence. The civil trial jury found in his favor. Specifically, the jury found that the store had restrained Cruz against his wishes and without legal justification, that his prosecution was instituted maliciously and without probable cause, and that Gibson's employees acted willfully, intentionally, and without regard to Cruz's rights. The jury awarded Cruz both compensatory and punitive (exemplary) damages.

On appeal, Gibson claimed several points of error. First, the store argued that the amount of the actual (compensatory) damages and punitive damages were excessive. The appeals court did not buy this argument, noting that Cruz had to post bond and hire an attorney, he had spent a night in jail, he had missed work, and the account of his arrest was published in the local newspaper, causing him considerable embarrassment. The court noted that Cruz was entitled to compensation for his loss of time, for physical discomfort, inconvenience, and physical and mental injury. In short, the amount of the actual damage award was correctly left up to the sound discretion of the jury. The punitive damages award equaled the amount of the actual damages. Again, the appeals court found that the award was not so large as to be unreasonable. There was no indication that the jury was prejudiced against the store or that evidence had been disregarded. As a result, the amount of the damages awarded was left intact.

Relative to the questions of probable cause, intent, and maliciousness, the appeals court also found that the evidence supported the jury's finding. Despite the hat being soiled, despite the fact that all of the family members reported the hat had been previously purchased, and despite the fact that no employee reported seeing Cruz remove the hat from a display, the store elected to prosecute. The court noted that there was evidence that the restraint was without consent or legal justification (cause). Further, the court noted that at trial, even after seeing the tape indicating the hat's purchase, an employee continued to state that she believed Cruz stole the hat. As a consequence, the court found that there was evidence of malice and that the employees had acted without regard to the rights of the plaintiff. Finally, the court noted that Gibson's employees never acknowledged that they might have made an honest mistake. The findings of the trial court were affirmed.

There must be probable cause to detain an individual. When probable cause does not exist, the protection offered by merchant detention statutes will fail to materialize. Store employees need to act on cause, professionally, and with an understanding that their actions may one day be subject to review.

In *Swift v. S. S. Kresge Company, Inc.*, the court, citing a previous ruling, noted that a corporation is "not liable for damages resulting from the speaking of false, malicious, or defamatory words by one of its agents, even where in uttering such words the speaker was acting for the benefit of the corporation and within the scope of the duties of his agency, unless it affirmatively appears that the agent was expressly directed or authorized by the corporation to speak the words in question." Thus, corporations normally are not to be held responsible for employees' remarks that may be slanderous. To hold otherwise would create significant liability and potentially chaos in the business world. Corporations and other businesses would be reluctant to hire people knowing that if they were to say something that someone found offensive, the corporation would be held accountable and potentially liable in each instance.

However, while corporations normally are not responsible for slanderous remarks by employees, *Swift* clearly shows that there are some circumstances where a corporation can be held liable for its employees' statements. Specifically, corporations can be held liable for slanderous remarks by employees where the corporation authorizes such remarks and, perhaps more ominous, gives its approval to the remarks by its actions. Affirmative actions by a corporation that indicate it gave authorization for such remarks or directed that such remarks be made on its behalf would, according to the citation just given, place a corporation in a situation in which liability for slander might accrue.

Murray v. Wal-Mart, Inc. is one of the few shoplifting-related cases to be tried in a federal court. The case's placement in the federal court system arose from the various claims of the plaintiff, which included, among other things, a charge that her constitutional rights had been violated. As in *Johnson*, it is an example of a store originally having the privilege to apprehend and detain an individual and then losing the privilege.

Murray successfully sued the store, claiming it and its employees had violated her constitutional rights, intentionally inflicted emotional distress on her from actions arising from her apprehension and detention as a shoplifting suspect, and pursued a malicious prosecution of her. Murray charged that the store's employees did all of these things despite the fact that the defendants did not find any evidence the plaintiff had shoplifted and therefore had no legal basis for their course of action.

Murray was accused of hiding a bottle of cologne in her halter top by an employee of Wal-Mart. That employee, along with the store's manager and assistant manager, detained Murray as she exited the store. Murray denied taking the cologne and pulled her halter top down to show that she was not concealing any merchandise within it. It was alleged that the manager then used profane and racially derogatory comments towards Murray, as he accompanied her to the second floor of the store. There, the contents of her purse were emptied onto the floor, revealing that no merchandise was concealed within the purse. Store employees then called police and requested prosecution of Murray. Murray was taken into custody and searched at the police station by a female police officer, who reported finding no merchandise concealed upon the plaintiff.

Perhaps not surprisingly to many, Murray was acquitted of wrongdoing at her trial on criminal theft charges, which was pursued by the store. Later, she sued Wal-Mart, the city, certain police officers who were involved in her arrest, and various employees of Wal-Mart. The United States District Court, Eastern District of Arkansas, found for Murray. The U.S. Court of Appeals, Eighth Circuit, upheld the district court's finding and assessment of $15,000 in actual damages, $10,000 in punitive damages, and over $7,000 in attorney's fees. The court noted that the store lacked probable cause to detain the customer or initiate prosecution after the customer showed she did not possess the bottle of cologne alleged to have been taken.

The word on which the preceding sentence revolves is the word "after." Prior to showing that she was not concealing store merchandise, the store employee may have had cause to believe Murray had hidden store merchandise in her top, and as a consequence, potentially had the right to investigate. Subsequent to Murray's actions, it appears that store employees had two opportunities at which the situation could have been brought to closure, and yet no such closure occurred. Once Murray showed that the store employee was wrong, that she was not hiding any merchandise as described by the employee, she should have been released. At the very least, one may argue that following the search of Murray's purse, again a search that proved fruitless, store employees should have released Murray. Finally, one may question the wisdom of prosecuting a criminal case for theft when there was no evidence that any store merchandise had been stolen.

One additional note on Murray's case which will be further discussed in Chapter 5 is the report that Wal-Mart employees' actions were not in keeping with established store policy. Again, it is important in the execution of any plan aimed at deterring shoplifting or related to the apprehension and detention of shoplifting suspects that employees have knowledge of store policy and that they are trained to follow the policy. Such is definitely a case where ignorance is not bliss. Ignorance of store policy and failure to follow a legally prescribed course of action may result in a civil judgment notwithstanding the existence of merchant protection statutes. A store must have a plan of action that meets expectations of state law, and employees should be expected to know the plan and adhere to it.

Again, the basis for an apprehension and detention is cause. One must have cause to believe that a shoplifting incident is occurring in order to exercise the conditional privilege offered merchants to apprehend and detain individuals. Without cause, a detention would likely be found to be illegal and subject to a civil action. Immunity from civil liability follows those situations where cause was shown to exist and where employees followed legal courses of action. So, what can "cause" one to believe a shoplifting incident has occurred? Can the sounding of an exit alarm be cause enough for one to believe that a shoplifting incident is occurring?

Technological advances in shoplifting deterrence have resulted in increasing numbers of stores equipping their exits with antitheft systems that trigger an alarm when sensitized tags are brought through the alarmed exit area. When used correctly, these sensitized tags and their alarm system counterparts have been shown to be effective in deterring some types of merchandise theft. As a result, many stores have come to rely on such systems to alert them to a potential shoplifting incident. In an ideal world, an alarm sounds and the shoplifter is exposed. After all, is the sounding of an alarm not a dead giveaway that a shoplifting incident is occurring? Well, as is often the case, the answer is yes and no.

In *Clark v. I. H. Rubenstein, Inc.*, the Louisiana Supreme Court had to rule on whether or not the tripping of an electronic sensor's warning was sufficient cause to suspect a person of shoplifting. Despite the existence of a strong merchant protection statute in Louisiana, the facts surrounding the case allowed the supreme court to find in favor of Clark.

Rubenstein's had reportedly been suffering substantial losses from shoplifting activities. In an effort to reduce such losses, the store installed an electronic security system which consisted of warning alarms at store exits and alarm-tripping tags attached to various pieces of merchandise. As is usual with such systems, store clerks were expected to remove the tags at the time of sale so as to prevent the alarm from sounding. If the tag was not removed and a piece of merchandise so tagged passed through the exit sensor, an audible alarm would sound and alert store personnel to a possible shoplifting.

At the time of Clark's detention, the system had been in operation for less than one week. Clark was reported to have made a purchase for which she dutifully paid the store. As she exited the store, an alarm sounded. A number of shoppers reported hearing the alarm and witnessing the following events.

1. One of defendant's employees followed Clark and asked her to return to the store.

2. Clark returned and allowed her parcels to be searched in view of other shoppers.

3. An item for which Clark had paid still had an alarm tag attached and was found in one of the parcels. It appeared that the clerk had failed to remove the tag from the item at the time Clark paid for the item.

4. Clark was then allowed to leave the store with apologies from the store manager.

The detention of Clark was of short duration. At no time during her detention did any of the store's employees accuse plaintiff of shoplifting. Store employees were reported to have treated Clark courteously during the detention.

Shortly after the incident, Clark filed suit against the store. Clark claimed that the experience was embarrassing and she was so upset that she took medication. The trial judge dismissed her claim. The appellate court affirmed the lower court's ruling, holding that the plaintiff had been lawfully detained under Louisiana's merchant detention statute. The Louisiana Supreme Court reversed the decision and remanded the case to the appellate court for a determination of damages.

In looking closer at the case, it is important to note that the court based its decision on the events that had transpired during the three days preceding Clark's detention. The court held that because the store's personnel were aware that the alarm had sounded on multiple occasions due to failures to remove tags by other clerks, the store did not have reasonable grounds to believe the sounding of the alarm was caused by a theft of goods by the plaintiff.

The court reasoned that since the store personnel should have known that the alarm was just another false alarm, they should not have approached and detained Clark as a shoplifting suspect. The decision at the time left little doubt that an alarm sounding was not in and of itself reason to believe a shoplifting incident was occurring, given that multiple false alarms had been sounded during the previous few days. Clark's detention should not have ensued.

Louisiana's legislature recognized the conundrum the ruling presented to retailers. If a retailer installed an electronic alarm system and responded to an alarm, yet still could be held liable for false detention, the installation of such an alarm system potentially becomes a liability, not an asset. On the other hand, if retailers failed to respond to an alarm sounding because they felt they could be held liable for such a response, then the question arises as to why such a system should be installed in the first place. Shortly after the ruling, and in direct response to the state's supreme court reversal in *Clark*, Louisiana's legislature amended the state's merchant detention laws to legislatively overrule the basis for the decision. Now the state's law allows that merchants who post notices to the effect that an electronic security system is in use shall, upon a signal from such a device, have reasonable cause to detain a person. By including in state law the proviso that an alarm sounding provides reasonable cause to detain an individual, given that sufficient notice has been provided warning of the presence of an electronic alarm system, the legislature again moved to assist merchants in their efforts to protect their property interests.

Several states have now followed Louisiana's lead and declared that the sounding of an electronic alarm provides a merchant with reasonable cause to detain individuals while maintaining the civil liability immunity offered by merchant detention statutes. It should be emphasized that the wording in the laws that gives merchants the privilege of detaining individuals due to the sounding of an alarm specifies that sufficient notice to customers informing them that a store uses electronic detection systems needs to be provided. As a consequence, a manager of a store that utilizes an electronic alarm system needs to be careful to assure that notices are posted around the store alerting shoppers to the presence and use of an electronic alarm system. Prominent notice of the presence of such systems must be in place for merchants to maintain the conditional privilege of apprehension and detention offered by merchant protection statutes. Failure to provide sufficient notice will leave a store vulnerable. Understanding and adhering to the law will protect a store.

In *Causey v. Katz & Bestoff, Inc.*, the plaintiff claimed she suffered damages during an alleged apprehension effort by employees of one of Katz & Bestoff's drugstores in New Orleans. The plaintiff sued, seeking recompense for purported actions she claimed were unreasonable and aggravated a preexisting emotional condition that manifested itself by causing her to become totally and permanently disabled. The suit claimed the disability would require the plaintiff to seek emotional and mental care on an ongoing, permanent basis. The trial court's dismissal of Causey's claim was upheld by the Court of Appeals for the Fourth Circuit of Louisiana. It is interesting but not surprising to see why, once the situation leading to the case was described.

The store where the incident took place is located in New Orleans. The plaintiff, accompanied by another individual, entered the store, shopped around, and then proceeded to leave the store without making a purchase. The K&B store in this case, like many chain drugstores, was equipped with an electronic detection system that would activate an alarm if tagged merchandise passed through the detectors located near the door. Upon checking out customers, clerks were to deactivate the electronic tags. Reportedly, the alarm sounded as Causey was preparing to exit the store.

Causey claimed that a store guard took her arm and escorted her to a back office where a store manager and a female employee were located. Her purse was emptied of its contents, and the pockets of the coat she was wearing were searched. Among her belongings was a product purchased previously at another store, which purportedly could have set off the alarm. Causey reported that there was a man exiting the store in front of her who ran away when the alarm sounded. Causey was detained for less than thirty minutes and released. The store did not initiate arrest actions against her. Shortly thereafter, Causey filed suit against the store and its insurer, claiming the incident aggravated a preexisting medical condition, resulting in her total disability.

The contrast between the plaintiff's testimony and that of store employees was puzzling. Store employees could not recall the incident as described by Causey. Indeed, the store's employees' accounts of the situation differed from the plaintiff's in a variety of ways. The incident was said to have taken place around lunch time. However, employee testimony indicated that guards were not on duty in the store until after 7:00 P.M. Further, the plaintiff claimed that the manager on duty at the time of the incident was a white male, while records indicated that the assistant manager, who is a black male, was on duty. Further, a log detailing alarm activations kept by the store did not include Causey's name. Despite the puzzling differences in the testimony, the court noted that Causey's detailed description of the incident and the procedures followed by store employees were consistent with K&B's store policy and procedures, and the case proceeded on that assumption.

Causey's suit did not claim that employees abused her in any manner. The suit did not claim that the electronic alarm system malfunctioned. Causey claimed not to have noticed any signs warning customers that an electronic alarm system was in use. She testified that defendants never accused her of stealing and that she was detained for around twenty-five minutes in the store. Causey did claim that the guard grabbed her arm and took her to the back of the store. It was this action that Causey claimed was an unreasonable use of force, since she had offered to allow her purse to be searched while still in the front of the store.

The court noted that Louisiana law allows for an authorized detention when the following conditions are met:

1. The detention is effected by a merchant, specially authorized employee of the merchant, or a peace officer.
2. There is reasonable cause to believe the person detained has committed theft.
3. Only reasonable force must be utilized in detaining the individual for interrogation.
4. The detention must occur on the merchant's premises.
5. Such a detention must last no longer than sixty minutes.

Further, as was noted earlier, pursuant to legislative action following the ruling in *Clark v. I. H. Rubenstein, Inc.*, Louisiana law stipulates that when electronic article surveillance is being utilized within a store and sufficient notice has been posted to that effect, a signal from such a system will constitute a sufficient basis for reasonable cause to detain a suspect. As one might surmise, the store's employees were acting within their privileged rights when they moved to detain Causey and investigate the sounding of the alarm.

In a case involving a major department store chain in Oklahoma, the U.S. Court of Appeals noted that Oklahoma law holds that the plaintiff in a case alleging wrongful detention must prove that a store lacked probable cause leading to a detention in order to recover damages. This was a major finding and is to be applauded by merchants, since to hold otherwise would have placed a major burden on retailers. In other words, under Oklahoma law, the plaintiff must prove the store lacked probable cause in order for the privilege of apprehension and detention not to hold and for the plaintiff to recover damages.

In this case, *Taylor v. Dillard's Department Stores, Inc.*, the plaintiff was stopped by two individuals identifying themselves as employees of a Dillard's store located in Bartlesville. It was reported that Taylor was stopped shortly after she left the store. The employees who suspected the plaintiff had shoplifted in the store questioned her for a short period of time, determined that she had not hidden a pair of jeans under the pair of jeans she had on, and allowed her to go on her way.

Shortly thereafter, Taylor filed suit, seeking $750,000 in damages for actions related to her detention, which, she argued, had been without just or probable cause. At the jury trial, Dillard's argued that its employees' actions, based on reasonable suspicion and probable cause, were justified. The jury, acting on instructions of the trial judge that the store must prove it had probable cause to detain Taylor, returned a verdict against Dillard's and awarded damages in the amount of $35,000.

Oklahoma's merchant detention statute is similar to statutes in other states. It allows a privileged detention by a merchant or the merchant's agent or employee when such a person has probable cause to believe that a theft of merchandise or money has taken place or is taking place. An apprehension should be for a reasonable length of time and conducted in a reasonable manner. Such apprehensions and detentions may be conducted for a variety of purposes, including the following:

1. The conducting of an investigation, including questioning, to determine whether there has been an illegal taking of merchandise or money.
2. Alerting law enforcement agents as to the facts relevant to the detention.
3. Conducting a reasonable search of the detainee and his or her belongings when there is reason to believe that the merchandise or money may be lost.
4. Recovering the merchandise or money alleged to have been illegally taken.

As do other merchant detention statutes, Oklahoma's law states that reasonable detentions conducted for these reasons shall not constitute an unlawful arrest or detention. Further, merchants and their agents or employees who conduct reasonable detentions for these reasons shall not be held criminally or civilly liable to persons so detained. Dillard's had argued that its apprehension and detention were conducted in a reasonable manner and were based on probable cause.

On appeal, Dillard's argued that the court's instruction as to the store's responsibility to prove probable cause was in error. The U.S. Court of Appeals for the Tenth Circuit agreed, reversed the decision, and remanded the case back to the lower court. The court of appeals, though, did not agree with the store's argument that it should have received a directed verdict in its favor. The store had argued it deserved a directed verdict since Taylor had not proven the store lacked probable cause. The court noted that whether or not probable cause existed was a question of fact for a jury to decide.

It is apparent that to enjoy the protection that merchant protection statutes offer during an apprehension and detention, a merchant must suspect the detainee of shoplifting. If there is no basis for a suspicion or if a suspicion ceases to exist, the person involved should be allowed to leave. When apprehension and detention become necessary, they should be conducted in a reasonable manner and according to state law.

Another incident of interest occurred in a grocery store when the manager observed an individual placing batteries into his coat pocket. In this case, *Schwane v. Kroger Company, Inc.*, Schwane had not yet passed the checkout counter of the store and, indeed, testified that he merely put two of the batteries into his coat pocket in order to free a hand so that he might look at magazines for sale on a rack, situated some fifteen feet from the registers. His other hand contained six additional batteries, according to Schwane, though there was conflicting testimony as to the number and placement of the batteries.

According to Schwane's testimony, the store manager approached him, grabbed him, and questioned him about what he had put into his pocket. He told the manager that he had put the two batteries into the pocket so that he might look at a magazine. The manager took Schwane to the office and allegedly accused Schwane of attempting to steal the batteries. The manager asked a store employee to watch Schwane as he called police to report the incident.

The police arrived a short time later and took Schwane into custody after hearing the report of the incident from the manager. Plaintiff was subsequently taken to the police station and booked. Schwane was not put in a cell but was allowed to remain in the office until his bond was posted a few hours later.

The trial was held a few weeks later. Testimony by Schwane indicated that he had not intended to steal the two batteries, that he had the money to pay for them, that he had six other batteries in his other hand, and that he was merely trying to facilitate looking at a magazine. The store manager testified as to the events as he saw them. In the end, Schwane was found innocent of the shoplifting charge.

Schwane sued for false arrest and malicious prosecution. A judgment was entered on behalf of the plaintiff, and Kroger appealed. The appeal centered around a question asked of the plaintiff during the trial about the impact the arrest would have on his future career opportunities, specifically regarding the likelihood that future employers would want to know whether or not he had ever been arrested. The Missouri Court of Appeals for the Kansas City District found the overruling of the objection relative to the question to have been in error and reversed and remanded the case for a new trial.

In short, this case emphasizes that not all actions by customers could or should be considered criminal in nature. There are true "lapses" in judgment or other such innocent occurrences where a customer may appear to be taking something but is not intending to defraud the store.

The author once surveyed district attorneys in one state about how they felt the shoplifting problem should be handled. It was interesting to note that even though district attorneys generally felt shoplifters should be prosecuted, they also felt that each case needed to be considered and pursued on its own merits. Specifically, there are many incidents in which customers, similar to Schwane, put merchandise in a cart, baby buggy, or a pocket innocently, without the intent to steal from the store. In those cases, and perhaps in others, prosecution may not serve justice and may only serve to place one's store at risk.

Indeed, one of the district attorneys surveyed described a personal situation similar to Schwane's, where he had been shopping in a variety store and when his hands were full, put a package of gum in a pocket to facilitate picking up another product. At the cash register, the district attorney paid for the merchandise with the exception of the gum in his pocket. He was in his car when he said he remembered the gum. Immediately, he ran back into the store and paid for the gum. He said the incident had really upset him, even though it was an innocent mistake. He mentioned that had he been seen putting the gum in his pocket and subsequently arrested for shoplifting, the publicity would surely have damaged his career. This particular district attorney emphasized that explanations and situations need to be evaluated before a decision to prosecute is made.

In *Jefferson Stores, Inc. v. Caudell*, the jury believed Caudell when she stated that she had meant to pay for the merchandise in question. In this case, Caudell was shopping in a Jefferson Stores location with her two young children. While shopping, she picked up a large key ring and took it with her and the children to the food counter, where they ate lunch. While there, and in view of the lunch counter waitress, she transferred her keys to the ring, mentioning to the waitress and another lady seated close by that she would not lose this ring. She removed the price tag and put it on a cigarette package that she constantly had in her hand. She then put the ring in her open purse. While doing this, Caudell was being observed by a store security guard. Returning to the store, Caudell and her children shopped for over two hours, making several purchases.

Caudell claimed that upon exiting the store, her arm was grabbed and she was turned around. At this, she dropped the package to the ground, and its contents spilled. She claimed that a pain ran through her arm and went down both legs. Another employee directed Caudell to return to the store. Once there, she was given a statement to sign and allegedly told that if she did not sign it, she would be arrested and her children taken into custody. Caudell claimed that her back began hurting; she had undergone three previous surgeries on her back. After she signed the statement, which was essentially a confession to shoplifting and a release of the store from liability, Caudell was allowed to leave. Reportedly, she was not allowed to pay for the ring and leave, ostensibly because the store's policy dealing with shoplifting negated that possibility. Subsequently, Caudell's reinjury to her back forced her to leave her employment and undergo additional treatment for her back injury, and according to her claim, Caudell ended up disabled. She sued the store for damages related to a false arrest, assault and battery, and personal injuries that she claimed she suffered as a result of the detention.

Florida's merchant detention statute (Fl. St. § 812.-015) is very clear in that it offers civil liability protection to a police officer, merchant, or merchants' employee who has "probable cause for believing that goods held for sale by the merchant have been unlawfully taken by a person and that he can recover them by taking the person into custody, [and the statute states that he] may, for the purpose of attempting to effect such recovery, take the person into custody and detain him in a reasonable manner for reasonable length of time." The act further states that such a taking into custody by a merchant or merchant's employee shall not render the merchant criminally or civilly liable for false arrest, false imprisonment, or unlawful detention. The point to note from this case, and again the point that is emphasized in its jury verdict, is that probable cause must exist in order to garner the protection the statute offers. Since testimony conflicted as to the existence of probable cause and reasonable detention, the jury was given the charge of deciding whether or not probable cause to detain Caudell had been present and whether or not the actions of the security guards had been reasonable.

The jury's finding for Caudell indicated that they believed the store guards had acted in an unreasonable manner. While one may argue that the guards had probable cause to detain Caudell for investigation, the jury apparently believed that the security guards' actions pursuant to the apprehension and detention were not conducted in a reasonable, lawful manner. Indeed, their finding for punitive damages indicated that they perceived the actions to be unreasonable to a fault. The store appealed. The District Court of Appeals of Florida, Third District, reviewed the case. The appellate court noted that the issue of reasonableness as it pertained to the detention was correctly given to the jury to ascertain. Reasonableness, as the issue related to the detention and to the time period during which Caudell was detained, was found to be lacking by the jury. The judgment of the trial court against the store was affirmed.

The case of *Williams v. F. W. Woolworth Company* is a case where actions and comments of the store's assistant manager were found to be unreasonable. In general, remarks made by store employees pursuant to a shoplifting investigation are privileged. That is, the store and the employees are offered civil liability protection when they have probable cause to detain and do so in reasonable manner.

In *Williams*, the plaintiff was stopped by the store employee after a cashier alerted him to the fact that she had seen Williams place candy in her shopping bag. The assistant manager approached Williams and inquired about the contents of her bag. She replied that she had some candies and some patterns she had purchased. The store employee then asked to examine the contents of the bag and reportedly Williams refused, stating that she would only allow the police to search her bag.

The assistant manager called a security guard for assistance. When Williams attempted to leave the store, he followed her and asked that she return. She complied and was taken to a back room. Once there, the guard searched her purse and shopping bag. The assistant manager stated to Williams that the store retained the right to search all handbags, directed her to the middle of the store, pointed out a shoplifting notice displayed in the store, and read it to her. The assistant manager left Williams with the security guard. Williams produced a receipt showing she had paid for the candy in her possession. The guard apologized to her and allowed her to leave.

Williams then sued, seeking damages for emotional distress caused by the actions of the store employees. Testimony by Williams claimed that she had been embarrassed by the store employees and that the assistant manager's escorting her to the middle of the store and reading her the shoplifting notice and other actions, which were conducted in view of employees and customers, some of whom she knew, were unreasonable and damaging. The trial court agreed, and the jury returned a verdict against the store. The appellate court affirmed the trial court's judgment, noting that the actions of the store's assistant manager were reasonable up until a point. Escorting the plaintiff to the middle of the store, reading her the notice, and other actions taken in the full view of employees and customers were deemed unreasonable, and as such were not protected by the merchant protection statute.

In another vein, store managers and security personnel know of individuals who, for a variety of reasons, usually associated with their being mentally incapacitated, take merchandise from a store without payment. Such taking is not done with an eye to defraud the store, but rather grows from the individual's lack of mental capacity or lapse in concentration. Oftentimes it is a better public relations gesture and smarter management action to ask the family of the individual for payment for the goods than to try to prosecute an individual with a mental deficiency. Prosecuting "little Johnny," who would never hurt anyone, who is the darling of the neighborhood, and whom everyone knows has a mental deficiency, for picking up a candy bar in a store and eating it will not teach little Johnny a lesson, nor will it win loyalty from customers in the neighborhood who learn that the store's manager had the gall to prosecute an innocent like Johnny.

Prosecuting can be and is a deterrent to shoplifting. However, prosecution must be conducted based on cause and should be conducted in an intelligent manner. Prosecuting each and every person who takes merchandise or is suspected of taking merchandise from a store without payment is not a smart move.

Among cases where a decision probably should have been made not to prosecute was a case where a 3-year-old child was seen taking a grape from a produce display and quickly eating the grape. This incident purportedly happened in the produce section of a grocery store, while the child was seated in a grocery basket and the mother of the child was placing produce in a bag. The manager of the store who witnessed the child's act insisted on pressing charges against the 3-year-old for retail theft. The child was caught red-handed; surely he is serving a long prison sentence. Yeah, right. The judge threw out the case, noting that a child who puts something in his or her mouth is committing a natural act. As many parents lament, young children often put things in their mouths, things that parents frequently wish they would not put in their mouths. In this situation, the judge realized the child was doing nothing more than what other young children are likely to do. It was an innocent act, not an overt act of stealing. The judge's statements indicated that he was sympathetic to stores relative to the shoplifting problem, but emphasized that he expected to see real shoplifters brought before him, not young children being themselves.

A manager desiring to bring a charge of shoplifting or other charges against an individual should base such charges on whether or not probable cause exists to pursue such a course of action. Lacking probable cause to detain an individual or, worse, charging an individual for a criminal offense without probable cause can place a store in civil jeopardy.

A case involving an investigation for shoplifting that did not result in a charge of shoplifting being levied but resulted in a suspect being charged with disorderly conduct helps shed light on the concept of probable cause. In the case of *Gaszak v. Zayre of Illinois, Inc.*, a security guard standing at one of the store's exits directed a customer (Gaszak) to use exits on the other side of the store. The guard's testimony charged that as the plaintiff walked towards the other exits, she stopped; removed merchandise from under her coat; placed the merchandise, identified as baby apparel, on a counter; and continued across the store. She then proceeded to a checkout line and, after waiting her turn, made a purchase. As she was exiting the line, the guard approached the plaintiff and informed her that the manager would like to see her. She agreed to go and see the manager. He testified that he escorted her to the office in a courteous manner and had no further conversation with her before arriving at the office.

Once in the office, Gaszak was questioned by the store manager and the guard. The plaintiff opened her coat to show that she was not hiding any merchandise. She denied trying to steal merchandise and became upset. After questioning the plaintiff for approximately one-half hour, the manager and guard told her she could leave. The guard reported that the plaintiff then exited the store and that as she drove away, she blew her horn and yelled vulgar words at him. Later, the guard went to the police and filed a complaint for disorderly conduct against Gaszak. No charge of shoplifting was levied.

A couple of days later, the police went to Gaszak's home and arrested her on the disorderly conduct charge. Reportedly, she went to court three times before the charges were dismissed, apparently for failure of the complainant to show. Subsequently, she filed suit against the store, the manager, and the guard. The plaintiff claimed she had been falsely arrested and maliciously prosecuted.

In the case that ensued, the plaintiff testified that she did blow her horn for a few seconds as she exited the parking lot. She denied using vulgar language but admitted she was upset by the incident. Further, she claimed that since her arrest, she had detected a change in her neighbors' attitudes towards her and her family. Indeed, one neighbor testified that the reaction of the neighborhood to the arrest was one of general unease and resulted in the neighbors treating Gaszak coldly and generally avoiding her.

At the conclusion of the trial, the court dismissed all of the defendants as to the charge of false arrest. Further, the charge of malicious prosecution against the manager was dismissed, but a judgment was entered against the guard and the store as to the charge of malicious prosecution. While the appellate court affirmed the finding on the malicious prosecution verdict, it reversed the ruling dismissing the false arrest charges, noting that the question of probable cause (or the lack thereof) was a question for the jury to decide.

At the center of the concern on the false arrest charge was the wording of Illinois's merchant detention statute, which states that a "merchant, his agent or employee, who has probable cause to believe that a person has wrongfully taken or has actual possession of and is about to wrongfully take merchandise from a mercantile establishment, may detain such a person in a reasonable manner and for a reasonable length of time for the purpose of investigating the ownership of such merchandise." The appellate court noted that the statute must be strictly interpreted according to the plain meaning of its terms. In other words, the courts are not at liberty to creatively interpret statutes that are clearly written. As such, a merchant may detain an individual only when there is "probable cause to believe [the] person has wrongfully taken or has actual possession of and is about to wrongfully take merchandise." Lacking probable cause, a detention poses risks.

In this case, the question of probable cause should have been presented to the jury. Conflicting testimonies mandate a juried resolution based on perceptions of witness veracity. The appellate court found the trial court erred in granting a directed verdict relative to the false arrest charge and remanded the charge of false arrest back to the lower court for further proceedings.

As noted, damages were awarded at the trial on the malicious prosecution charge. The elements considered relative to the amount of damages included the mental suffering of the plaintiff, injury to the plaintiff's reputation, and the plaintiff's attorneys' fees. These items were considered in arriving at the judgment, which was upheld by the appellate court. The court noted there was evidence in the record not only to justify the verdict but to suggest the jury acted within the trial court's instructions.

The jury did not award Gaszak punitive damages. The awarding of punitive damages is possible only when willful and wanton conduct is shown to have existed in the efforts of the defendants. Apparently, the jury found that the defendants' actions wronged the plaintiff but that the actions were not serious enough (willful and wanton) to warrant the awarding of punitive damages.

As stated in *Bonkowski v. Arlan's Department Store*, "a store employee who reasonably believes that a person has unlawfully taken goods held for sale in the store has a privilege to detain the person for reasonable investigation of the facts. Such a privilege is a common-law defense to common-law tort of false arrest." The statement from this case is clear as to its meaning. When a store employee has probable cause to believe someone is stealing goods from the retail store, the employee has the privilege of detaining the individual for the purpose of investigating the situation. Again, as long as probable cause exists, a store employee and the store will be protected by merchant detention statutes, so long as the detention and investigation are conducted in a reasonable manner.

In this case, besides suing for false arrest, the plaintiff sought damages for defamation. Individuals who have sued for damages in shoplifting-related investigations often claim they are embarrassed and humiliated. There is no denying that being stopped by a store employee and/or standing in a doorway while an alarm sounds can be embarrassing. That is why professionalism and courtesy should be a part of every investigation scenario. Still, while an "embarrassment" is often impossible to prevent, it too can be protected under merchant detention statutes.

In the case of *Conn v. Paul Harris Stores, Inc.*, Conn entered a Paul Harris Store located in Indianapolis. At approximately the same time that Conn entered the store, another individual reportedly entered and exited the store. Simultaneously, a merchandise alarm sounded at the front of the store. Employees chased the individual who exited the store but failed to apprehend him. Upon returning, an employee mentioned to the store manager that Conn had entered the store at the same time as the individual who left.

Shortly thereafter, a police officer who was working part-time for the shopping center as a security guard went to the store and talked with the manager. The manager pointed out Conn to the officer and mentioned that an employee had seen Conn enter the store at about the same time as the individual that employees had chased had entered the store.

The officer then went to Conn, asked if she knew the shoplifter, and requested Conn's identification. Conn replied that she did not know the shoplifter, reportedly refused to supply identification, exited the store front, and entered the mall. Once in the mall, Conn reportedly uttered an obscenity and accused the officer of singling her out because of her race. Conn was then arrested on a disorderly conduct charge of which she was acquitted at trial. Subsequently she filed suit against the city of Indianapolis, the corporate owner of the mall, and the store. It was reported that she settled her claims against the city and the mall. A summary judgment Conn sought against the store was denied.

Conn's appeal of the adverse summary judgment regarding her claims of false imprisonment, slander, and malicious prosecution asserted that the store lacked probable cause to believe she had participated in a theft and therefore was wrong in identifying her to the officer. Specifically, she claimed that the trial court erred in not granting her a summary judgment, since the issue of whether or not the store manager possessed probable cause to detain her for shoplifting was in dispute. Paul Harris Stores argued that it never detained Conn, and therefore, any assertions that it lacked probable cause to detain her were moot. The store emphasized that the officer was not an employee of the store and that Conn was never detained until her arrest on the disorderly conduct charge. The store, asserting that its employees did not apprehend and detain Conn for shoplifting, did not seek protection under Michigan's merchant detention statute. Instead, it relied on the argument that its employees were providing the officer with factual information and as such were not responsible for his actions.

In reviewing the facts of the case, the concept of false imprisonment was reviewed. False imprisonment, it was noted, is an "unlawful restraint upon one's freedom of locomotion or the deprivation of liberty of another without his consent." The facts concerning the store employees' actions, the actions of the police officer/guard, the exiting of the individual who apparently had set off the alarm, and the events that followed were described similarly by all parties. In reaching a decision on the false arrest charge, the court noted that Conn herself noted that the officer was not an employee or agent of the store. Since the actions that led to the filing of the suit could not be interpreted to imply that store employees had restrained or detained Conn in any manner, it is not surprising that the store was not seen as being so callous as to arrive at a summary judgment on the charge of false imprisonment.

Relative to the charge of slander, Conn again failed in her attempt to have the lower court's refusal to issue a summary judgment overturned. In arriving at a conclusion on the slander charge, the appeals court noted that if an individual directs the attention of a police officer to a supposed breach of the peace and the officer arrests the individual for a crime committed in his or her presence, then the person who did nothing more than communicate facts to the officer is not liable for false imprisonment, even if the arrest is later found to be unlawful.

Merely stating to an officer what one knows of an alleged crime but not making any charge or request as to an arrest does not make oneself liable in an action for illegal arrest. Specifically, when an individual seeks the assistance of a police officer and details his or her version of the facts to a police officer, leaving it up to the police officer to determine an appropriate response, and the individual does not interfere in the intelligent exercise of the officer's discretion, then the mere relating of facts as one understands them does not in itself give rise to liability. The store manager reported to the officer what she knew. The officer, with that information, sought to question Conn. Only after she refused to supply identification and became uncooperative did he arrest her on a disorderly conduct charge. Conn was never accused of retail theft, nor was she arrested for such.

In determining whether or not a statement is defamatory, its impact on the reputation of another must be assessed. If a statement is seen as harming the reputation of another to the point that such reputation held on the part of the community has been lowered or if the reputation has been harmed to the extent that others are deterred from associating with an individual, then defamation has probably occurred.

For the purpose of making its point, Paul Harris Stores posited that even if the statement to the police officer was slanderous (a position it obviously disagrees with), the statement would be protected by statutory privilege. Statements made to police officers in good faith pursuant to a criminal investigation are made in the performance of a duty to the public, and are thus privileged. Still, as was noted, the privilege extended to merchants is a conditional privilege. Merchants must act in accordance with the law, and without malice, in the performance of their duties in order to benefit from the protection offered by the law.

To show malice, a plaintiff must show that the privilege was abused by excessive publication of the information, by use of the occasion for an improper purpose, or by a lack of belief or a lack of grounds for believing that what was said was true. The court noted that Conn failed to show that the publication was not legally justified, that the occasion was used for an improper purpose, or that the manager lacked grounds for believing that what she reported to the police officer was true. It was Conn's burden to set forth the specific facts showing a genuine issue pertaining to a question of malice, and the court noted that Conn's effort fell short in such regard. Absent a showing that the store manager acted outside the purpose of the privilege, the trial court acted properly in granting summary judgment to the store on the charge of slander. The trial court's finding for the store's request for a summary judgment was affirmed by the Court of Appeals of Indiana.

Volume Shoe Corporation was sued for damages when a customer was arrested after visiting a Payless Shoe Store owned by the corporation. In *Lipari v. Volume Shoe Corporation*, Lipari was said to be shopping in the store and trying on shoes. She had sought and received assistance from an employee and a manager of the store. According to her testimony, while looking at a pair of shoes, Lipari remembered that she had left a roast cooking in her oven. She placed the pair of shoes she was looking at on the bench or the shelf, she could not remember which, and left the store.

Shortly thereafter, the store employee noticed an empty shoe box on the shelf. She reported it to the manager, and the two quickly looked around and did not locate the shoes that should have been in the box. A quick review of the register tape indicated that the shoes had not been sold. The two quickly concluded that Lipari had taken the shoes. The manager had the employee go out to the parking lot and write down Lipari's license plate number as she was driving away. The police were called and given the plate number, a description of Lipari, and a report of the incident. The responding officer took a report and asked the employee to sign a form indicating whether or not the store intended to prosecute the suspect for shoplifting. Ostensibly, after checking with the manager, who confirmed they would prosecute, the employee signed the form.

Police went to Lipari's residence and took her to police headquarters for questioning. A detective again confirmed with the store that it desired that Lipari be prosecuted. Lipari was booked, jailed, and released after her husband posted bond. At her criminal trial, no one appeared to testify against her, and the case was dismissed. Her suit against the store's corporate owner for malicious prosecution quickly followed.

At the civil trial, Lipari was awarded $13,000 in actual damages and $74,000 in punitive damages. The store appealed. As was seen in *Conn v. Paul Harris Stores, Inc.*, employees reporting truthfully and in good faith facts to the police, when they allow the police to investigate and arrive at their own conclusion as to whether or not to arrest an individual, do not normally expose themselves to civil liability.

In the case of *Lipari*, though, Lipari was identified by the store employees as the "culprit." Her license plate number and her description were given to the police. The police were given an indication that the store wanted Lipari to be prosecuted. This is a different manner of reporting the crime than that noted in *Conn*, since the police reporting form was signed indicating that the store wished to prosecute. Despite their investigation, or perhaps regardless of it, testimony by the police officers involved indicated that the store wished to prosecute Lipari for the theft of shoes. Indeed, testimony by a police officer indicated that the prosecution would not have been initiated had it not been for the insistence of the store manager.

Malicious prosecution is said to exist when a person is identified as a culprit in a crime and legal steps are taken to prosecute that person despite the fact that probable cause for prosecution does not exist. The court noted that a reasonable jury could have inferred that the store was guilty of malicious prosecution in view of the evidence, which supported the charge that the employee reported the license number and personal description of Lipari as a shoplifter and indicated to police that the store wished to prosecute Lipari in particular. This was not seen as a case where information was furnished to police officers and the police were allowed to come to their own conclusions based on a thorough investigation, despite the store's argument that it had not directed the police, expressly, to arrest and charge Lipari.

As one might assume by now, the appellate court upheld the lower court award of actual damages of $13,000. The awarding of punitive damages had also been contested. The court noted that the actions of the employees were based on suspicion, not probable cause. Due to the size of the corporate owner and the finding that the store employees' actions were based on suspicion, not probable cause, the punitive damage award of $74,000 was not seen as excessive and was allowed to stand.

An incident in a grocery store led to the filing of a suit alleging damages from the apprehension and detention of an individual arising from that individual's removal of a baby bottle nipple from the store display. In *Jorgensen v. Skaggs*, Jorgensen went shopping at a grocery store. She was accompanied by her infant child and two friends. She reportedly removed a baby bottle nipple from a shelf, placed it on the end of one of her fingers, and used it to entertain her infant while she shopped. Jorgensen entered the checkout line with the nipple on her finger clearly in view. She purchased and paid for a basket of groceries. While leaving the store, Jorgensen was met by a security employee of the store, who asked that she return to the store. In the store, she was reportedly detained for ninety minutes and questioned, first by store employees and later by a police officer. No criminal charges were filed against Jorgensen as a result of this incident, and subsequently she filed suit for false arrest, false imprisonment, malicious prosecution, defamation of character, and assault and battery.

The civil trial judge granted summary judgment in favor of the store, apparently accepting the store's argument that there were no genuine issues of material fact and that the store was immune from civil liability under the state's (Utah's) merchant detention statute. Jorgensen appealed the granting of summary judgment in favor of the store. On appeal, the state's merchant detention statute took center stage. Utah's statute, like similar statutes in other states, allows that merchants who possess reason to believe that merchandise has been wrongfully taken by an individual and that recovery of the merchandise is possible by taking the individual into custody may take that individual into custody and detain the individual, for the purpose of attempting such recovery or for the purpose of informing a police officer of the circumstances leading to the detention. Further, Utah's statute is explicit in stating that such a detention, when conducted in a reasonable manner and for a reasonable length of time, shall not render the merchant civilly or criminally liable for false arrest, false imprisonment, slander, or unlawful detention. The only time a merchant may accrue liability under Utah's law (UT ST § 77-7-14) is when it is shown that a "custody and detention are unreasonable under all the circumstances." In other words, as long as a detention is predicated on probable cause, is reasonable, and is conducted in a reasonable period of time, the merchant is protected. When there is no cause, the detention is unreasonable, and it is conducted for an unreasonable period of time, the merchant may be held liable.

In this case, the appellate court noted that there were still factual disputes that needed to be resolved—specifically, whether the detention was conducted in a reasonable manner and completed in a reasonable period of time. The appellate court noted that these factual disputes had to be settled prior to the establishment of statutory immunity. Citing the conflicting accounts as to the reasonableness of the detention as a central tenet of its actions, the appellate court reversed the summary judgment in favor of the store and remanded the case to trial.

Detentions must be based on probable cause to believe the crime of shoplifting is occurring or has occurred. Given that probable cause to detain exists, then a store employee must assure that the detention is conducted in a reasonable manner and for no longer than a reasonable period of time. In *Jorgensen*, the state's statute is clear as to expectations of reasonableness. Reasonableness must prevail "under all the circumstances" in order for a store to garner protection under merchant detention statutes.

In a case involving an electronic alarm system, a married couple sued Sears, Roebuck & Company after the wife was detained and had her packages searched by Sears employees. In this case, *Parker v. Sears, Roebuck & Company*, Mrs. Parker was exiting the store when an audible alarm sounded and a red flashing light, which was part of the alarm system, became activated. She was escorted by Sears employees to a counter, where her packages were emptied. Employees discovered that an electronic alarm tag had accidentally been left on an item Mrs. Parker had purchased. Parker became upset, returned her purchases, and left the store.

Subsequently, the Parkers sued Sears, seeking medical expenses and general damages. The Parkers claimed that the store's audible and visual alarm system had drawn unnecessary attention to her, that the actions of employees further embarrassed her, that employees had made no attempt to alert those in the immediate vicinity that the alarm had sounded by accident, and that employees made no attempt to explain to onlookers that no crime had been committed.

Sears employees testified that notices are posted at each store exit alerting customers to the fact that an electronic alarm system is in place. The store proffered that employees' actions were reasonable during the apprehension and detention. The detention was brief and did not approach the state's statutory limit of one hour. The apprehension and detention were initiated by the sounding of the alarm system, which under the state's statute, is seen as probable cause to initiate action. Given this, the store sought and received a summary judgment from the district court. In short, the summary judgment dismissed the Parkers' claims.

The Parkers appealed the granting of the summary judgment. For a summary judgment to be granted, it must be shown that no genuine issue of material fact exists and that reasonable minds would conclude that one is entitled to such a judgment as a matter of law. The Court of Appeals of Louisiana, Second Circuit, reversed the district court judgment and remanded the case back to the district court. The appeals court noted that the allegations that the store's alarm system drew unnecessary attention to the plaintiff and that employees failed to explain to onlookers that the plaintiff was not guilty of a crime as suggested by the alarm system were issues of material fact. Since issues of material fact were present, a granting of summary judgment should not have ensued.

In many cases, it may be argued that careful attention to detail and simple courtesy can go a long way to prevent scenarios such as was seen in *Parker*. The sounding of alarms due to the failure of employees to remove electronic alarm tags does nothing in the way of developing customer goodwill. Employees need to be trained to remove all such tags. Vigilance on the part of employees charged with removing electronic tags is a must. While most customers who are embarrassed will never file suit, the goodwill lost cannot be estimated. The old retailing axiom that says a happy customer comes back and an unhappy customer tells friends of the unhappiness holds much weight. Employees need to take extra care in environments where electronic tags are in use.

The bad news is that employees, especially newer ones, will always be prone to accidents. Alarms that create embarrassing situations may always be with us. The good news is that electronic technology continues to march on. Increasingly, tags that don't have to be removed but are immediately desensitized upon scanning or by their placement on a desensitizing countertop are gaining favor in retail stores. Such point-of-sale desensitizing of alarm tags will undoubtedly reduce the number of false alarms.

And finally, on this note, simple courtesy can go a long way in preventing bad situations. There can be no denying that apprehensions and detentions are capable of creating embarrassing situations. Professionalism, courtesy, and, it may be argued, discretion need to be instilled in all employees. Employees should keep in mind that if the situation were reversed and it was they who were being apprehended and detained, they would not want to be embarrassed, especially when they have done nothing wrong.

In this regard, the author recently purchased a bottle of shampoo from a drugstore that has an electronic alarm system. The clerk, a high school–age male, forgot to desensitize the alarm tag. Consequently, as the author exited the store, the alarm sounded. There were two other customers in the immediate vicinity who witnessed the author stopping and holding up his bag in the direction of the clerk. The clerk yelled he was sorry, that he keeps forgetting about the tags, and said just to keep walking, as he waved the author towards the door. No embarrassment. No detention. Just a clerk admitting he made a mistake and assuring the author that he should just keep walking out the door. Courtesy and common manners go a long way in many situations.

A form of shoplifting that injures stores as readily as taking merchandise without any payment involves the taking of merchandise without proper payment. Indeed, switching price tags in order to purchase merchandise at a price lower than that which is sought by a store is a widespread form of shoplifting, impacting especially among stores that have not yet moved to electronic scanning. In response to this form of shoplifting, some retailers have switched to price tags that shred or fall apart when removed, making switching more difficult. The increasing utilization of nonitem pricing coupled with the continued adoption of affordable electronic scanners is reducing the incidence of tag switching in some types of retailers, primarily grocery stores. Finally, retailers are taking greater care to secure price guns and price tag blanks so as to minimize such switching by employees and others with access to the guns. Granted, a problem with price guns is that they are readily available from large discount stores that service the retail trade. This makes their total control difficult but is an area to which retail executives need to direct some of their concern.

It should be noted that price tag switching with an intent to defraud a store is a form of larceny and, like shoplifting, is illegal. When probable cause exists to detain a person intending to steal from a store through tag switching, a store will undoubtedly find itself in the same situation as with a person detained for outright theft of retail merchandise.

When an investigation and detention revolve around the issue of tag switching, it is imperative that probable cause exist to detain, that the detention be conducted in a reasonable manner, and that it be concluded in a reasonable period of time, Lacking probable cause, a detention for tag switching will leave a store, its employees, and its agents vulnerable to civil damage awards. Detentions to investigate tag switching that are based on the existence of probable cause and conducted in a reasonable manner and for a reasonable period of time will undoubtedly be viewed as privileged. Lacking these factors, an investigation is unlikely to be deemed to have been privileged, and thus such an investigation will not garner the civil liability protection offered through merchant detention statutes. Store employees need to be aware that just because someone brings up a piece of merchandise that has an erroneous price tag does not mean that the person who is attempting to buy the product put the wrong tag on the product. Indeed, the fact that retail employees have been known to erroneously price merchandise should surprise few, if any. Therefore, possession of a product with a wrong tag, in and by itself, does not, and should not, automatically equate to wrongdoing on someone's part.

The case of *Moore v. Target Stores, Inc.* is a case that involved allegations of tag switching and one in which the jury found the argument that probable cause existed and was the basis for the investigation to be lacking. Accordingly, the store and its agents (a private security firm contracted by the store) were found liable for damages, allegedly incurred by Moore.

Moore's testimony indicated that she went shopping for toys at a Target store. She purchased a toy telescope. As she walked to her car, she was approached by an individual who identified himself as a security officer for Target and asked that she return to the store. Moore returned to the store, was advised of her constitutional rights, and was accused of switching price tags. The police were called. A police officer arrived on the scene quickly and took Moore into custody. Moore claimed that these actions and accusations were conducted in plain view of numerous people, including some acquaintances.

It should be emphasized at this point that information on the case did not indicate that anyone actually saw Moore switch price tags. The only thing apparently observed by anyone was that Moore purchased a toy telescope that had a "lower than normal" price contained on the wrong tag.

As might be surmised, Moore eventually sued Target and its security provider. Evidence presented included testimony that indicated it was not unusual for items in the Target store to contain multiple price tags. Ostensibly, when prices changed, new tags simply were placed over existing tags. Target's employees testified that items for sale did often contain multiple price tags. Indeed, one store item presented as evidence by Moore was shown to possess nine price tags.

As has been noted elsewhere in this book, it was the plaintiff's (Moore's) responsibility to prove lack of probable cause. Considering the evidence she presented, the testimony of the store's own employees, and her testimony, the jury found that the security guard and the store lacked probable cause to detain and arrest Moore. The Court of Appeals of Oklahoma, Division Number 1, affirmed the trial court judgment in the amount of $15,000 in compensatory damages and $35,000 in punitive damages. The appellate court noted that Moore's purchase of a product with the wrong price tag did not establish probable cause to believe that she had switched the tag. The jury's finding that there was no probable cause to detain Moore and the affirmation of the trial court judgment probably surprised few.

Again, this case points up the need for store employees to establish a detention and an arrest on probable cause. The fact that something is priced wrong does not indicate that someone switched the price tag. It could have been switched by another customer. It could have been erroneously priced by a store employee. Whichever, the fact that someone attempts to buy merchandise from a store and the price tag is not correct does not, in itself, establish probable cause. Indeed, sometimes store employees compound another employee's error. In one such incident, the author was shopping at a grocery store when a gentleman ahead of the author at the checkout counter purchased a six-pack of German beer. The clerk rang up $1.50 for the purchase. The customer pointed out to the clerk that it had to be an error—that the beer was much more expensive than the amount indicated. The clerk acted indignant and said that the beer's price was correct—that the scanner did not make mistakes. The customer asked to have his purchase held so that he might return to shop some more, and the clerk agreed. Moments later, the customer reentered the line with a basket full of German beer. Mistakes occur. Make no bones about it.

A reasonable detention must be based on probable cause. It must be conducted in a reasonable manner. It must be concluded in a reasonable period of time. If a detention is seen to lack probable cause, reasonableness relative to actions taken or to the amount of time necessary to investigate will be lacking. If probable cause does not exist, then reasonableness does not exist. Again, store employees need to base their actions on probable cause. Lacking such, they should not initiate a detention.

Some state statutes make detentions a little easier to call, as they statutorily declare that concealment of goods can be considered evidence of willful concealment on the part of the customer, and as such, stores are privileged to investigate. For instance, in *Safeway Stores, Inc. v. Gross*, it was seen that Arkansas's state merchant protection law specifies that concealment of retail goods is prima facie evidence of willful concealment. Persons who are found to be willfully concealing merchandise are subject to detention, in a reasonable manner and for a reasonable length of time, for the purpose of recovering these goods. Detentions for shoplifting are to be viewed as privileged and as such will not subject the individual initiating such a detention civilly liable for false arrest, false imprisonment, or unlawful detention.

A department store prevailed in its efforts to control shoplifting losses when an individual filed suit following his detention for possible shoplifting. The case of *Gabrou v. May Department Stores Company* arose as a result of an incident in which Gabrou was apprehended, detained, searched, and arrested for allegedly shoplifting a pair of gloves. The gloves were found in his possession. At his criminal trial, Gabrou was acquitted by the jury. His suit against May Department Stores sought damages for false imprisonment, malicious prosecution, assault and battery, and the intentional infliction of emotional distress. The superior court delivered a directed verdict in favor of the store, and Gabrou appealed.

Background information revealed that Gabrou, while shopping in the store and after selecting and paying for several items, sought to purchase a shopping bag the store sold via machines located near the exits. It was purported that one such machine did not work for Gabrou, so he went to another. While trying to retrieve a bag from the second machine, Gabrou reportedly put a pair of gloves into his pocket in order to free a hand to remove the bag. Gabrou had not paid for the gloves. According to Gabrou's testimony, he was approached by a security employee of the store, who gave him a shopping bag. The conversation that followed arguably may have been unclear, or at least contested, but centered on whether Gabrou had paid for the items in his possession. Gabrou replied in the affirmative and was then asked to stand near an alarm detection device. It is disputed as to whether it sounded, but Gabrou reported that he asked about paying for the gloves, stating he had not yet finished shopping. The security guard took Gabrou to the office, where he was searched, questioned, and turned over to the police. At his criminal trial, Gabrou was acquitted.

In his suit against the store, Gabrou sought recompense for damages arising from his detention and arrest. For Gabrou to have prevailed on the false imprisonment claim and his claim of malicious prosecution, the store would have had to fail to show that its employees lacked probable cause to apprehend Gabrou. The store proved to the court's satisfaction that it did indeed have probable cause to detain Gabrou. Possession of probable cause is a defense against charges of false imprisonment and malicious prosecution. The court noted that Gabrou had stated that he had paid for the items in his possession, that the alarm sounded when he stood near the detection device, and that only then did he concede that he perhaps had not paid for all of the items in his possession.

Relative to his claims that he had been the victim of assault and battery and that the store had intentionally inflicted emotional distress on him, the court disagreed. To prove assault and battery, Gabrou would have had to have shown that the store exercised a degree of restraint that would be described as being excessive in its ability to maintain the detention. The state's merchant detention statute allows the use of "reasonable force" to detain an individual. The use of force greater than that, which one might ascribe as being excessive, was not proven to the court's satisfaction. Given that the use of reasonable force was seen as having been present, the claim alleging assault and battery and the claim that the store intentionally inflicted emotional distress were not bought into by the appellate court. The appellate court affirmed the lower court's finding that the store employees acted with probable cause and in a lawful manner.

Again, it will be seen many times in dealing with shoplifting that probable cause must exist as a basis for apprehensions and detentions. Given that probable cause exists and that detentions are conducted in a reasonable manner and for a reasonable period of time, stores and their employees will garner the protection that merchant detention statutes offer.

Oftentimes, shoplifting suspects are employees of stores. What about situations dealing with suspects who are employees? Does a merchant need to possess probable cause to detain and question an employee relative to a shoplifting incident? Should merchants exercise reasonableness in detaining and interrogating employees they suspect have shoplifted merchandise from the store? One must be concerned with whether the same level of care is afforded employees as is afforded non-employees who are suspected of shoplifting.

A situation in which an assistant store manager was called in by store security, questioned, and searched resulted in the store manager filing suit against the store following the individual's termination of employment by the store. The assistant manager's (Ruffin's) employment was immediately terminated following his detention and interrogation by store security personnel. Ruffin's suit for damages alleged he was the victim of a false imprisonment (*Lansburgh's, Inc. v. Ruffin*).

At his civil trial, he testified that a customer had come into his shoe department to exchange a pair of boots in her possession for which she had no sales receipt. He reported giving the customer a store slip marked "no sale" so that she could leave the store without being bothered by security. The customer returned a week later to exchange the boots and was referred to the department manager. Since the department manager had left the area, the customer was assisted by another manager. Eventually, Ruffin was called to the security office, and he went there.

Ruffin reported that at first he thought he was called to the security office as a normal manner to deal with a customer's problem. He had been there previously in dealing with shoplifting cases involving others, was familiar with the office, and did not feel he was being detained. Eventually, though, he was questioned by security personnel as to his sales practices. Security reviewed his department's sales records and noted that there was no indication that payment had been forthcoming for the boots, nor had there been a cash overage, which, ostensibly, one might expect had a sale been made and not entered on the cash register. Ruffin reported that he was questioned for over two hours by security personnel but was never threatened by them in any manner.

Security personnel purportedly asked if Ruffin would want to cover the cash deficit (pay the cost of the boots), but he refused. Eventually, Ruffin was told he would be booked, was ordered to empty his pockets, and was searched. No incriminating evidence was found. Ruffin was escorted to the personnel office, where he was notified that his employment was being terminated. No criminal charges were filed, and he was allowed to leave the store. These events, as reported by Ruffin, were the basis of his suit for false imprisonment. A request by the store for a directed verdict in its favor was denied. The civil court jury awarded Ruffin $13,000 in compensatory damages and $25,000 in punitive damages. A request by the store for a judgment notwithstanding the verdict was also denied. The store appealed.

The District of Columbia Court of Appeals reviewed the case. Its review hinged primarily on the question of probable cause and whether or not a detention had taken place. On the question of the detention, the appellate court agreed with the trial court that a detention did occur, albeit late, in the questioning of Ruffin. Specifically, at the point Ruffin was told he would be booked, was ordered to empty his pockets, and was searched, the detention was initiated. The question then that begs to be asked is whether or not probable cause existed to have initiated the detention.

As is noted elsewhere in this text, probable cause related to false imprisonment and illegal detention is a question of both law and fact. When facts are in dispute, it is up to the jury to ascertain the true facts surrounding the situation, based on the evidence presented. However, in reviewing the case, the appellate court noted that despite conflicts in testimony surrounding the questioning and detention, there was evidence that there was probable cause to detain the plaintiff in a reasonable manner and for a reasonable period of time.

In other words, among the points of contention, the plaintiff claimed the detention lasted over two hours and that the guards were armed. The store claimed that the detention was of a shorter duration and that the guards were not armed. Still, these differences in the testimony have no bearing on whether or not probable cause existed to detain Ruffin. If probable cause existed to detain, then the request for a directed verdict for the store should have ensued, since there were no other charges made other than that the plaintiff had been falsely imprisoned (without cause).

The court noted that the security personnel had received information that the plaintiff had supplied no sales slip for the purchase and, after further investigation, had reason to believe that the proceeds of the sale had been misappropriated by the plaintiff. Armed with such relevant information, the security personnel had probable cause for the detention. The court ruled that the detention that ensued was conducted in a reasonable manner and was reasonable in duration. Accordingly, the appellate court found that there was no factual issue for a jury to consider relative to the existence of probable cause and that the evidence established the existence of probable cause as a matter of law. Since the evidence established the existence of probable cause as a matter of law, a directed verdict for the store should have ensued. The trial court's judgment was reversed, with instructions to enter the judgment in favor of the store.

Whether an individual is an employee or a customer, the existence of probable cause is paramount when pursuing a detention. With probable cause, a merchant who pursues a reasonable detention will be protected by merchant protection statutes. Lacking probable cause, a merchant will be at risk.

Table 3.1
Citations and Management Implications in Chapter Three

Case	Implication
Johnson v. Schwegmann Brothers, Inc., 397 So.2d 868 (La.App. 4Cir. 1981)	Probable cause to detain a suspect is a must. If probable cause does not exist or ceases to exist, then the privilege to apprehend and detain does not exist or ceases to exist.
Hardin v. Barker's of Monroe, Inc., 336 So.2d 1031 (La. App. 1976)	When probable cause ceases to exist, the immunity from civil liability offered by merchant detention statutes ceases to exist.
Shaw v. Rose's Stores, Inc. and R. M. Faw, 205 S.E.2d 789 (N.C.App. 1974)	There must be a basis, cause, for a merchant to pursue an apprehension.
Robinson v. Wieboldt Stores, Inc., 433 N.E.2d 1005 (Ill.App. 1982)	Once probable cause ceases to exist, the store no longer has the privilege to detain. Punitive damages are usually not awarded against corporate defendants for acts committed by employees. Exceptions to the rule concerning punitive damages may arise when the corporation ratifies or affirms the acts in question.
Tweedy v. J. C. Penney Company, Inc., 221 S.E.2d 152 (Va. 1976)	Unless punitive damages are sought, malice does not have to be proven in order to recover in an action claiming malicious prosecution. Compensatory damages may be obtained for insulting words or malicious prosecution without an actual showing of malice.
Gibson Discount Center, Inc. v. Cruz, 562 S.W.2d 511 (Tex.App. 1978)	Probable cause must exist in order to acquire statutory protection. Punitive damages may be awarded when employees act intentionally and without regard to the rights of the individual.
Swift v. S. S. Kresge Company, Inc., 284 S.E.2d 74 (Ga.App. 1981)	Corporations normally are not responsible for slanderous remarks made by employees, even if the remarks can be said to further the corporation's interest. However, corporations may be held responsible if they affirm the comments through their behavior or actions.

(Continued)

Table 3.1 (*Continued*)

Case	Implication
Murray v. Wal-Mart, Inc., 874 F.2d 555 (8th Cir. 1989)	Probable cause must exist to apprehend and detain an individual. When a sound store policy exists, employees need to follow store policy. Pursuing a prosecution without cause may result in liability.
Clark v. I. H. Rubenstein, Inc., 25 ATLA No. 1 (1982)	The sounding of an alarm does not mean someone is guilty of theft. However, most states now allow that if warnings are posted stating that electronic surveillance is in place, the sounding of an alarm creates sufficient cause to allow a privileged investigation.
Causey v. Katz & Bestoff, Inc., 539 So.2d 944 (La.App. 4Cir. 1989)	The sounding of an alarm, in stores with public notices to the effect that detection systems are in place, serves as sufficient basis (reasonable cause) to pursue a reasonable investigation.
Taylor v. Dillard's Department Stores, Inc., 971 F.2d 601 (10th Cir. 1992)	Oklahoma law requires that plaintiffs prove the lack of probable cause in order to recover damages. Whether probable cause exists or not is a question to be decided by a jury.
Schwane v. Kroger Company, Inc., 480 S.W.2d 113 (Mo.App. 1972)	Managers need to use prudence in decisions concerning prosecution.
Jefferson Stores, Inc. v. Caudell, 228 So.2d 99 (Fla.App. 3Dist. 1969)	A detention must be conducted in a reasonable manner and concluded in a reasonable amount of time. Lacking reasonableness, a store will find itself vulnerable. A jury will decide the issue of reasonableness.
Williams v. F. W. Woolworth Company, 242 So.2d 16 (La.App. 4Cir. 1970)	Actions that are deemed unreasonable will not be protected as merchant privilege. Remarks made in public may be deemed to be slanderous. Lack of reasonableness may leave a store vulnerable.
Gaszak v. Zayre of Illinois, Inc., 305 N.E.2d 704 (Ill. App. 1Dist. 1973)	Lacking probable cause, a detention creates potential liability. Stores should not pursue prosecutions without probable cause.

Table 3.1 *(Continued)*

Case	Implication
Bonkowski v. Arlan's Department Store, 162 N.W.2d 347 (Mich.App. 1968)	A merchant who reasonably believes a person has unlawfully taken goods for sale has the privilege to detain the person for a reasonable investigation of the facts.
Conn v. Paul Harris Stores, Inc., 439 N.E.2d 195 (Ind.App. 1982)	Communicating factual information to a police officer in a nonmalicious manner and, in the presence of the officer, allowing the officer to make a decision to arrest an individual for committing a crime does not create a liability under Indiana law.
Lipari v. Volume Shoe Corporation, 664 S.W.2d 953 (Mo.App. 1983)	Malicious prosecution of a suspect may occur when a person is identified as a culprit and legal machinery is set in place to prosecute the individual. Lacking probable cause, a finding of malicious prosecution may be easily arrived at by a jury. A finding of malicious prosecution may result in the awarding of punitive damages.
Jorgensen v. Skaggs, 668 P.2d 565 (Utah 1983)	Under Utah law, a merchant who has probable cause to believe that retail crime is being committed and believes that he or she can effect the recovery of the merchandise involved can detain, in a reasonable manner for a reasonable period of time, the individual involved, for the purpose of recovering the merchandise and calling police. Given probable cause, merchants enjoy civil immunity unless the "custody and detention are unreasonable under all circumstances."
Parker v. Sears, Roebuck & Company, 418 So.2d 1361 (La.App. 1982)	When issues of material fact exist, then summary judgments cannot ensue. Stores using electronic alarm systems need to post such notices, and employees need to be vigilant about removing or desensitizing electronic alarm tags.

(Continued)

Table 3.1 (*Continued*)

Case	Implication
Moore v. Target Stores, Inc., 571 P.2d 1236 (Okla.App. 1977)	Probable cause must exist to garner protection for a detention. This is true when merchandise is stolen or when price tag switching is suspected. Initiating a detention without probable cause places a store at risk.
Safeway Stores, Inc. v. Gross, 398 S.W.2d 669 (Ark. 1966)	Some state statutes specifically declare that simple concealment of goods is evidence of willful concealment, and this assists stores in their efforts to garner the protection the law offers.
Gabrou v. May Department Stores Company, 462 A.2d 1102 (D.C.App. 1983)	Probable cause is a defense against the charges of false imprisonment and malicious prosecution. For a charge of assault and battery to stand, the force used to detain must be shown to have been excessive. Reasonable force to detain is allowed. The intentional infliction of emotional distress can also be dependent on the use of excessive force. Reasonableness must prevail.
Lansburgh's, Inc. v. Ruffin, 372 A.2d 561 (D.C.App. 1977)	When an employee is detained for shoplifting, one must exercise the same degree of reasonableness as would be exercised when dealing with nonemployees. Probable cause must exist to detain employees. When the existence of probable cause is determined as a question of law, a directed verdict should ensue.

SUMMARY OF CONCEPTS IN CHAPTER THREE

1. The conditional privilege to apprehend and detain persons suspected of shoplifting is predicated on the basis of sufficient cause.
2. A store owner or employee must possess reasonable cause or probable cause to effect a detention and garner protection under merchant protection statutes.

3. If probable cause does not exist or ceases to exist, then the protection offered by merchant detention statutes does not ensue or ceases to ensue.

4. When probable cause ceases to exist, detentions and investigations should cease.

5. Only persons for whom reasonable suspicion exists to suspect they are shoplifting or have shoplifted should be detained.

6. Normally, corporations are not responsible for slanderous remarks made by employees, but they may be held responsible when the corporation authorizes the remarks or affirms the remarks.

7. The sounding of an electronic alarm may initiate probable cause to detain if sufficient notices to the effect that an electronic alarm system is in use are posted in the store.

8. Store owners need to recognize that not all who fail to pay for merchandise intended to steal it.

9. Merchant detention statutes that are clearly written will be strictly interpreted by the courts. Courts will not creatively interpret statutes so as to arrive at some kind of equitable solution.

10. The awarding of punitive damages is possible when the conduct of store employees is shown to have been willful and wanton.

11. Reporting facts to a police officer, who then is free to investigate and proceed as the officer thinks best, does not necessarily impart liability on the part of the merchant.

12. To prove malice, a person must show that the privilege to detain was abused by excessive publication of the information, by the use of the occasion for an improper purpose, or by a lack of belief that what was said was true and factual.

13. Malicious prosecution is said to exist when a person is identified as a participant in a crime and legal steps are taken to prosecute the person despite the fact that probable cause for a prosecution does not exist.

14. Professionalism and courtesy should prevail when handling a situation in which shoplifting may be involved.

Chapter Four

Lawful Detention

An apprehension and detention of a shoplifting suspect must be legal in order for a merchant to claim the protection offered by merchant protection statutes. The apprehension and detention must be lawful. In other words, such detentions must be reasonable. At first glance, this notion appears hard to violate, given the conditional privilege merchants enjoy. However, there are many instances where store employees and managers have placed their employers at substantial risk by violating this principle. Illegal (unreasonable) searches of suspects can void the conditional privilege merchants enjoy and can make an apprehension unlawful. Unrestrained use of force can make a detention unlawful. An illegal search can make a detention unreasonable. A detention must be lawful, or civil immunity offered by merchant protection statutes will fail to materialize.

In a relevant case, *Mahon v. King's Department Store, Inc.*, the plaintiff had purchased a pair of blue jeans from the defendant. The day after she purchased the jeans, Mahon, wearing the jeans, returned to the store for additional shopping. After paying more than $100 for her purchases, Mahon was approached and stopped by the manager, who had been notified by an employee that she had seen the plaintiff leaving a fitting room area wearing a new pair of jeans. Additionally, the employee reported finding an old pair of jeans hanging on a nearby rack.

The manager took Mahon to the security office for questioning. There, the plaintiff denied stealing the jeans she was wearing and offered to telephone her husband to have him bring the previous day's receipt, which would prove she had purchased the jeans. Since the store had an aggressive policy of prosecuting every shoplifting suspect and since the policy denied phone calls to suspects until after the arrival of police officers, the manager refused Mahon's request to call her husband to have him bring the receipt. Instead, he called the police and formally filed a complaint, resulting in the plaintiff's arrest for shoplifting.

Ostensibly to preserve the jeans as evidence, Mahon was allegedly ordered by store employees to remove her jeans and to put on the jeans that had been found hanging on the rack. Mahon complied by removing her jeans and putting on the pair of old jeans. Reportedly, the old jeans were two sizes too small, and as a result, Mahon could not zip them up. Police arrived and, upon receiving the complaint, took Mahon into custody. She was handcuffed by the police and then led through the store wearing the unzipped jeans, past onlookers. She was then taken to jail, where she was booked for larceny.

Perhaps not surprisingly, at the close of the state's evidence on the criminal charge, Mahon's criminal case was dismissed. Shortly thereafter, Mahon filed suit against the store. Her suit contained a variety of charges, including false imprisonment, false arrest, and malicious prosecution. The jury in her civil suit returned a true verdict on the charges listed and awarded Mahon $40,000 in compensatory and punitive damages.

Another case sheds light on the expectations of reasonableness as it relates to searching a suspect's clothing. In *Bryant v. Sears, Roebuck & Company*, Bryant was required to remove her slacks in the presence of store employees to prove she was not hiding merchandise. No merchandise was found, and she was released. Bryant then sued for false arrest and slander. The jury returned a verdict of over $70,000 in compensatory and punitive damages. Merchant detention statutes do allow searches of handbags, baby buggies, shopping bags, and other items in the possession of individuals when there is probable cause to believe a theft has occurred or is occurring. The law does not allow searching inside a person's clothing or ordering individuals to undress so that they might prove their innocence. Again, such searches, if they are necessary, will be conducted by appropriate police officers as part of the booking process, when charges are filed. Store employees need to keep constant surveillance of individuals who have been detained for hiding merchandise under their clothing until police arrive. Employees should not order individuals to undress, nor should they search under clothing for merchandise.

In still another case involving the disrobing or partial disrobing of a suspect, a high school student successfully sued City Stores Company for damages after she was apparently forced to partially disrobe in the store's security office. In that case, *City Stores Company v. Gibson*, Gibson sued for damages, claiming she had been the victim of a false arrest and false imprisonment and, further, that the store had maliciously prosecuted her. Gibson, who alleged that she was required to partially disrobe in front of a female security guard after being taken to the security office, was arrested and spent a night in jail. She sued City Stores after her acquittal on shoplifting charges.

The jury awarded Gibson $5,000 on her complaints for humiliation, physical and mental suffering, and damage to her reputation. The trial court refused to change the damage award and denied a motion for a retrial. On appeal to the District of Columbia Court of Appeals, the judgment of the lower court was affirmed. The appellate court noted that while the damages awarded might seem high, the amount was not unreasonable. Further, the appellate court noted that the denial of the request for a retrial was correct, given the arguments presented.

One thing should be clear by now: allowing a suspect to disrobe or, worse, ordering a suspect to disrobe in order to prove his or her innocence is not a recommended action. Merchant detention statutes do not give merchants and their employees the right to disrobe or order the disrobing of suspects. To do so places one's store and oneself in a liability situation.

Merchant detention statutes are specific as to who may conduct the actual apprehension and detention in shoplifting situations. In many states, merchants, their employees, and their agents are protected by the conditional privilege intrinsic to such statutes. In still other states (such as Nebraska), only the merchant or his or her employees enjoy protection from civil damage awards under the statutes. In practically every state, the conditions under which an "arrest" is made vary among the classes of individuals conducting the arrest (i.e., law enforcement officer or citizen-merchant).

In *Cervantez v. J. C. Penney Company, Inc.*, it was seen that California law requires different levels of cause from a police officer than from a citizen in order to conduct an arrest in a shoplifting incident. For police officers, California law requires only that probable cause exists to make a warrantless arrest of an individual suspected of shoplifting. On the other hand, California law allows a citizen (merchant, employees, or agents of a merchant) to make a warrantless arrest of a shoplifting suspect only if the crime was actually committed in the presence of the citizen or the crime was attempted in his or her presence. These different levels of cause played a significant role in this case.

To demonstrate the impact of the state law on *Cervantez*, a little background information is required. In this case, a police officer working as a store security guard during his off-duty hours apprehended and arrested Cervantez on the basis of probable cause. The court noted that probable cause would justify such an arrest only if the officer was acting in his official capacity as a police officer and not in his capacity as a guard (agent) of the merchant. The plaintiff successfully argued that the officer was acting as a citizen (agent of the store) at the time of the incident and that probable cause was not sufficient to arrest him.

In the case of *Wilson v. Wal-Mart Stores, Inc.*, it was noted that "reasonable cause" for investigatory purposes is something less than "probable cause." The overriding purpose of merchant detention statutes is to allow merchants to conduct their business affairs and protect their property interests without fear of civil suits for actions taken in good faith.

In *Wilson*, the store was found to have followed a reasonable course of action, which was initiated when a store security guard observed Wilson and another individual hiding clothing under one of the women's skirts. The guard maintained constant surveillance of the women until they left the store. He then approached them and asked that they return to the store in order to be searched, and they complied. The pair was escorted into the invoice office in the rear of the store. The guard requested that a female clerical assistant search the two women. The store's general manager and the guard waited outside of the office while the store employee stayed to search the women. The door was left cracked, and the employee followed the guard's instructions on how to search the women. It was reported that the female employee, who had not conducted such a search prior to this incident, was very nervous. The assistant reported finding no clothing under the women's garments but later admitted that due to her inexperience with shoplifters, she had not maintained constant surveillance of the subjects. When no clothing was found, the two women were allowed to leave.

On entering the office, the guard found a bundle of clothing on the floor under a desk next to where the women had been standing. The guard attempted to catch up with the women but succeeded in catching only Wilson. It was reported that she offered to pay for the clothes.

In their suit, the plaintiffs argued that Wal-Mart did not have reasonable cause to detain them. They further argued that Wal-Mart did not conduct the investigation in a reasonable manner. The jury decision in favor of the store was affirmed on appeal. The court noted that Wal-Mart's employees had reasonable cause to believe a theft had been committed. According to the court, the "search must be reasonably related to the purposes of the detention and conducted in a reasonable manner." The manner of the apprehension and the search did meet those criteria.

An important point to mention, and one that will not be lost on many security managers, is that the security guard maintained constant surveillance of the women during the time they were in the store and as they exited. This constant surveillance is necessary to assure that a clean apprehension is conducted. In this litigious age, it is not unheard of for an individual to fake an incident with the hope of striking it rich in the courts or, just as worrisome, for an individual who is shoplifting to dump or pass off the merchandise to another in order to avoid prosecution. Store personnel should know that once an individual is suspected of shoplifting, they need to maintain surveillance of the individual while simultaneously summoning assistance from the manager, security, or other employees.

Another case in which the reasonableness of an apprehension was brought into question was the case of *Coblyn v. Kennedy's, Inc.* In *Coblyn*, the court noted that a store employee must use reasonableness in assessing whether or not probable cause exists. Lacking a degree of reasonableness in supporting one's actions and, as a consequence, failing to prove the presence of probable cause to initiate an apprehension and detention will leave one vulnerable.

This case grew from an incident in which a store guard observed Coblyn tying an ascot around his neck as he exited Kennedy's. Coblyn was approached by two store employees, one of whom was a store security guard; had his arm grasped by the guard; and was ordered to return to the store.

Reportedly, the store employee who initiated the apprehension of Coblyn did not see him take the ascot from a store display. Indeed, it was reported that Coblyn purchased a sport coat on the second floor of the store and left it in the store for alterations. He then proceeded towards the exit on the first floor. Prior to his leaving the store, Coblyn was observed removing an ascot from his pocket and tying it around his neck. The ascot was clearly visible to onlookers. Coblyn reportedly made no attempt to conceal it, nor were any of his actions necessarily suspicious in nature. The only potentially suspicious activity involved Coblyn's removing the ascot from his pocket and tying it around his neck as he exited the store.

After approaching Coblyn, the guard, who was accompanied by another store employee, ordered him to return to the store. Coblyn agreed and returned to the second floor of the store where he had purchased the coat. Along the way, he complained of chest pains. The sales clerk who sold Coblyn a coat was concerned when he saw Coblyn returning, approached the guard, and inquired as to the situation. Upon having the situation explained to him, the clerk confirmed that Coblyn had just purchased a coat and, more important, that the ascot in question did indeed belong to Coblyn.

As Coblyn looked weak, the store's nurse was called to the scene. Showing concern, she took Coblyn to the first aid office and gave him a soda tablet. Continuing to feel ill, Coblyn eventually was hospitalized. Later, charging that the guard's actions constituted false imprisonment and that he had been harmed as a result, Coblyn filed suit against Kennedy's, seeking recompense.

At trial, Kennedy's failed to demonstrate that the actions of its employee involved in the apprehension were reasonably justified in light of the so-called prudent man doctrine. In other words, the employee had not observed Coblyn taking the ascot from a display. The employee had not seen Coblyn attempting to conceal the ascot. It appears that the guard had only observed Coblyn tying an ascot around his neck as he exited the door. The ruling of the court leaves little doubt that lacking reasonableness in an apprehension, an apprehension will be seen as unlawful and a store will find itself at risk. A doctrine of reasonableness is seen to apply in many areas of merchant detention law and as such should serve as a basis for developing store policy.

Indeed, in one such case, a customer purportedly signed a confession admitting to taking goods without payment and then turned around and sued the store for, among other things, conducting the investigation in an unreasonable manner. In the case of *Mapes v. National Food Stores of Louisiana, Inc.*, the customer also claimed that the store lacked probable cause to have apprehended and detained her.

In this case, Mapes sued for damages arising from actions taken by store employees relative to the alleged shoplifting incident. In *Mapes*, the store's security guard testified that he observed Mapes put a box of antacid in her purse, observed her pass through the checkout area without removing the antacid from her purse, and continued to observe her as she left the store. He checked with the cashier to confirm that the customer had not paid for the item. He then approached Mapes in the parking lot, verified that she had the item, and asked her to return to the store.

Once in the store, he took her to the store's break room, where the contents of her purse was emptied onto a table. There were other employees present who witnessed the purse's being emptied and saw a box of antacid and four bottles of meat marinade among its contents. In the presence of store employees, Mapes is said to have signed a statement admitting she took the box of antacid without paying for it. Police were summoned to the store, and Mapes was taken to the station for booking.

Shortly thereafter, Mapes filed suit against the store alleging damages. Specifically, she claimed that there was no reasonable cause to detain her for questioning and that the investigation was conducted in an unreasonable manner. Relative to the first charge, that there was no reasonable cause to detain her, the court found otherwise. As was noted, the security guard observed her put the item into her purse, observed her during checkout, verified that she had not paid for the item, pursued her into the parking lot, ascertained that she did have possession of the item, and asked that she return to the store. As noted by the court, probable cause existed. The initial detention was allowed under Louisiana's merchant detention statute.

As for the complaint that charged the investigation was conducted in an unreasonable manner, the court again found for the defendants. It was noted that the charge of unreasonableness grew from the plaintiff's claim that the store employees refused to listen to her excuse for not paying for the merchandise. Specifically, the employees were said to have ignored her statements that she had not intended to steal the merchandise. Mapes charged that she was purposely humiliated despite her offering a reasonable explanation for her actions.

The court disagreed. It noted that Mapes had signed a statement admitting to taking the merchandise without payment and that her complaint centered on the store employees' refusals to investigate further her statements concerning her intent not to steal the goods. The court noted that there was no way to verify Mapes's state of mind. Despite her charge that the store's employees wrongfully failed to investigate her intent further, Mapes did not show any illegal treatment by her detainees during the investigation. Her appeal resulted in an affirmation of the finding by the trial court, which ruled that the detention was privileged (i.e., protected under Louisiana's merchant detention statutes) and that the store's failure to further investigate her insistence that she had not intended to steal the merchandise was reasonable under the circumstances.

In both *Lerner Shops of Nevada, Inc. v. J. P. Marin* and *Black v. Clark's Greensboro, Inc.*, it was seen that the submission to the mere verbal direction of another, unaccompanied by force or threats of any character, does not constitute a false imprisonment. False imprisonment is a serious restraint of one's liberty. It is an action that can result in damage awards. It is generally conceded to be a restraint of one's liberty without sufficient cause. It is paramount that a merchant possess probable cause to detain before initiating an apprehension and that the merchant follow the specifics of state merchant protection statutes if the store is to be protected from civil suits.

Hales v. McCrory-McLellan Corporation indicated that the presence and support of a police officer in an unlawful restraint does not legitimize the restraint. The court emphasized that force or coercion can take many forms other than direct physical contact.

Purportedly, while in the process of returning merchandise to the store for exchange, Hales was stopped and ordered by Morphis (a store employee) to accompany him. Hales did not have a receipt for the merchandise. Morphis directed another employee to call police. When the police arrived, Morphis indicated to them that he would "sign the papers." Hales was taken to the police station, detained until posting bond, and released. Hales was officially charged with shoplifting upon the filing of Morphis's statement in the recorder's court. Hales subsequently offered evidence of her innocence. Later she sued the store and its employees for illegal detention and false arrest.

The defendants contended that Hales had not been placed under arrest by them. They stressed that no force was exerted in detaining

Hales in the store, that she was not restrained in any manner while in the store, and that she accompanied the police to the station of her own free will. A restraint must be voluntarily consented to or it must be lawful. The court noted that calling a police officer to assist in a restraint does nothing to legitimize an unlawful restraint. Further, the presence of force or the implied threat of force by the police, when it compels a person to remain where the person does not wish to remain or to go where the person does not wish to go, is an imprisonment. The state's supreme court reversed the lower court's finding for the store and found for Hales. It was noted that in the case of an unlawful arrest, not only the individual defendants but their principal, the corporation itself, may be held civilly liable.

A case involving actions taken to investigate the potential theft of cash, not merchandise, resulted in the store manager investigating the purported theft while maintaining immunity from civil liability. In *Martinez v. Goodyear Tire & Rubber Company*, the store manager was shown to have legally detained an individual under the Texas merchant detention statute, although the property reportedly stolen was cash, not retail merchandise.

Background information indicated that Martinez drove her car to the Goodyear garage to have the oil changed. Purportedly, while seeking a seat in the store, she passed an open cash drawer while the manager had his back turned. Shortly thereafter, he turned to Martinez and told her the oil change bay was open. After receiving directions to the restroom, she proceeded to it. When Martinez returned from the restroom, the manager asked that she stay in the store because he suspected she had taken money from the open register. The manager then called for police assistance. A policewoman arrived, took Martinez to the restroom, searched Martinez, and found no money. Reportedly, Martinez was in the store from 5 P.M. until around 6:30 or 7:00 but was never questioned by the store manager.

At the trial, seeking damages, Martinez admitted on cross-examination that she never refused to wait. She stated that she was waiting for the oil change and, as a result, had not intended to leave the store. She did not refuse being searched and was never threatened with bodily harm. There was no evidence that she tried to call anyone for help.

The rule cited by the court was that if an individual voluntarily agrees with a request to remain and establish innocence, the act of staying does not produce the elements necessary to establish a false arrest. The specifics of Texas's merchant detention statute were cited. This statute provides, "A person reasonably believing another has stolen or is attempting to steal property is privileged to detain the person in a reasonable manner and for a reasonable period of time for the purpose of investigating ownership of property."

It is important that a store develop a policy detailing expectations as they relate to the actions of employees during apprehensions and detentions. The policy should follow the specifics of state merchant protection statutes. Such a policy and adherence to such a policy can prevent a store's having to pay damage awards.

Most of the cases cited in this book, and indeed most of the cases alleging damages resulting from apprehensions inside a store, purportedly occur at the hands of an employee or employees. That is, employees, while on duty, are alleged to have pursued some course of conduct that damaged individuals apprehended within the store. Every now and then, a case arises that alleges damages from an individual who was not an employee or was an employee who was off duty. Who is responsible when an off-duty employee or nonemployee apprehends and detains individuals within a store, especially when such apprehensions are unreasonable and, as a consequence, illegal?

The question as to a store's liability from the acts of its employee when he or she is off duty at the time of an incident arose in the case of *Rusnack v. Giant Foods Inc.* In *Rusnack*, a customer and an off-duty security officer were involved in a scuffle that resulted in Rusnack being handcuffed by the security guard, detained for police, and arrested. Oddly, the case did not involve a suspected shoplifter, but rather an altercation between the two that resulted in a shopping cart being pushed into the off-duty guard as he stood in the checkout line at the grocery store. Despite the fact that the case is not related to shoplifting, the liability of the store in such a situation is relevant to merchant risk exposure, thus it is briefly described here.

Rusnack, a customer, was shopping at a Giant Store situated in Rockville, Maryland. While he was in the checkout line, his basket reportedly bumped into another individual ahead of him. Rusnack claimed that the bumping was accidental and that the force involved was no stronger than one would normally use to push a cart into position in line. The individual claimed that the basket hit him multiple times and that he was responding to an assault with the basket.

Witnesses and both individuals involved described ensuing events similarly. The individual turned around, grabbed Rusnack, and proceeded to handcuff him. The two scuffled and fell to the floor. Rusnack, apparently bewildered by it all, kept demanding to see some identification. The scuffle resulted in Rusnack's face being bloodied, his ankle being twisted, his sustaining bruises in multiple locations, and his enduring pain from the use of the handcuffs. Rusnack claimed that the individual identified himself as a store security guard and quickly displayed an identification of some sort. Rusnack was detained for police and given over to their custody. Later, the individual preferred charges against Rusnack.

At the criminal trial for assault and battery, Rusnack was found not to be guilty of the charges. Subsequently, he sued the store for actions taken pursuant to his arrest. At the civil trial, the judge entered a directed verdict in favor of the store. The Court of Special Appeals of Maryland affirmed the trial court's finding that the store was not liable for actions taken by the off-duty security guard and ordered court costs to be paid by the appellant (Rusnack). As was noted, the security guard was acting on his own behalf. He was off duty and was employed at another location when on duty, and as a consequence he was not acting as an agent of the store but as a private citizen. To have found the store liable, the plaintiff would have had to have shown that the security guard was acting on behalf of the store and with the store's interest in mind. As was noted, even if the guard had been authorized to protect his employer's property and maintain the peace therein when off duty, and regardless of what precipitated the scuffle and arrest, the notion that he was actuated by the purpose of serving his employer's interest did not logically ensue. The guard was a shopper and acting in his own interests, not that of his employer. Since both parties involved in the scuffle were shoppers, the court's finding that the store was not liable for the scuffle and the injuries sustained by Rusnack should surprise few.

As stated earlier in this book, a large portion of stolen merchandise is taken by employees. Therefore, retail executives are, and need to be, especially wary of opportunities that may lead to employee theft. Because of the many opportunities that may lead employees to steal, retailers pay close attention to such theft. And, as one may expect, some of the suits against retailers filed by individuals apprehended and detained for allegedly shoplifting have been filed by employees. One such case involved Montgomery Ward & Company, Inc.

In the appeal of *Montgomery Ward & Company, Inc. v. Keulemans*, the appeal by the major department store chain, one of its security guards, and his supervisor failed to reverse a trial court's awarding of damages to a store manager (Keulemans) for actions arising from an incident in which the manager was arrested for shoplifting. In this case, the explanation of the manager to the security guard went unheeded, and the manager was arrested, later tried, and found innocent of retail theft. The suit by Keulemans sought compensatory damages and punitive damages. Both were awarded.

The background information for this case reveals that Keulemans's job responsibilities as manager of receiving regularly required him to audit price information on goods offered for sale and sometimes to remove from store shelves goods that were found to be improperly marked. Such goods were then taken to the receiving/marking area, and they would then be re-marked with the correct pricing information.

On one particular day at work, a guard with approximately one year's experience observed Kuelemans standing in front of a rack of sunglasses holding three pairs of glasses. While the guard was observing Kuelemans, Kuelemans was paged and directed to answer a phone. The guard watched as Kuelemans placed two pairs of the glasses onto the rack, deposited the third pair in a pocket, and went to answer the page. Later, after leaving the store, the security guard approached Kuelemans in the parking lot and asked that he return to the store. Once in the office, the guard accused Kuelemans of stealing a pair of sunglasses, a charge Kuelemans quickly denied.

Kuelemans explained that the pair he had in his pocket had been purchased at another nearby store and that he was just comparing the store's offerings with the pair he had already purchased. When he was paged, he placed the store's glasses back on the rack and put his in his pocket as he left to answer the page. By phone, the guard's superior indicated that he could not listen to Kuelemans's explanation, indicating instead that he was bound to listen to the guard's explanation of the incident. Later, Kuelemans's attorney and the guard went to the nearby store, where a manager there reported that they no longer sold the type of glasses that was reportedly purchased by Kuelemans.

Shortly thereafter, Kuelemans surrendered to police and was charged with shoplifting. Kuelemans was suspended without pay from work pending a trial. At the trial, two of Ward's employees testified that Kuelemans had worn sunglasses to work the morning of the incident. Further, an employee of the store where Kuelemans said he purchased the glasses testified that she had sold him the glasses at an earlier date. She was able to be specific as to the date of the purchase because she remembered his buying the glasses on a day he had brought film to be developed, and his name and the date had been recorded in the store's photographic logs. As one may surmise, Kuelemans was found innocent of the shoplifting charges.

Kuelemans's suit against Ward's and the other defendants quickly ensued. Kuelemans charged the store, the guard, and his supervisor with committing several transgressions, including false arrest, false imprisonment, malicious prosecution, and defamation. He was awarded compensatory and punitive damages. Ward's and the others appealed.

The supreme court considered a variety of arguments before arriving at its conclusion. For the purposes of this discussion, the question as to the existence of probable cause is paramount. The awarding of punitive damages can only be justified in such cases when actual malice is shown to exist, where malice may be implied, or from want of probable cause in a case for false arrest. The supreme court noted that based on the facts of the case, the jury could find that the guard lacked probable cause to arrest Kuelemans, since reasonable grounds to suspect Kuelemans was shoplifting did not exist. In short, it appears that the guard should have listened to Kuelemans's explanation and investigated the incident with that knowledge prior to initiating an arrest. Thus, lacking probable cause, the detention was unlawful, and the store and its employees were at risk.

As noted elsewhere, merchant detention statutes allow for the privileged apprehension and detention of individuals when probable cause exists to believe those individuals either committed retail theft or were in the process of committing retail theft. Reasonableness must prevail during detentions, and the expectation of such reasonableness is paramount. Many cases have hinged on whether the actions of store employees were deemed reasonable or not deemed reasonable by a jury. One question centers around what activities during an investigation are deemed reasonable and what activities are not deemed reasonable.

As could be surmised in the judgment associated with *Mahon v. King's Department Store, Inc.*, having suspects undress and exchange their clothes probably was deemed unreasonable, given the circumstances of that case. Having suspects undress or searching within their clothing is generally not protected as privileged under merchant detention statutes. In addition, at least one state, New York, prohibits the fingerprinting of suspects during detentions held for the purpose of investigating retail thefts. Indeed, New York's statute (NY GEN BUS § 218) states that a detention pursuant to a shoplifting investigation "shall not authorize the taking of such person's fingerprints at such vicinity unless the taking of fingerprints is otherwise authorized by section 160.10 of the criminal procedure law and are taken by the arresting or other appropriate police officer." Simply stated, New York's law makes it clear that store owners and their employees are not authorized to fingerprint suspects.

The prohibition against fingerprinting suspects was a point of consideration in the case of *Johnson v. Bloomingdale's*. In *Johnson v. Bloomingdale's*, the judge set aside the jury verdict for the store and ordered a new trial on the issue of damages. On appeal, the appellate court affirmed the lower court's judgment, holding that New York's merchant protection statute did not authorize the fingerprinting and photographing of customers.

As background to the case, Johnson was observed putting on a hat and then walking into another department of the store. The guard who observed Johnson reported that the plaintiff was twenty-five feet into the next department and appeared headed towards the door. At the time Johnson was stopped, a price tag said to be affixed to the hat was no longer on the hat. Johnson testified that he had an unpurchased hat in his hand when he stepped into the adjoining department to find his companions and show them the hat.

The guard requested that Johnson accompany him to the security office. Johnson complied, went to the office, and was searched. The guard then verified the price of the hat with the men's department and presented forms for Johnson to sign. Johnson was then photographed, fingerprinted, and released. Johnson was not charged with any criminal offense. The statute clearly provides that for any action for false arrest brought by a person detained on the retail premises, it "shall be a defense to such action that the person was detained in reasonable manner and for not more than a reasonable time to permit such investigation or questioning." The trial court's finding that the photographing and fingerprinting of Johnson exceeded reasonableness as it applied to such a detention was affirmed by the appellate court.

In Chapter 3, the case of *Gabrou v. May Department Stores Company* indicated that for a plaintiff to win on a claim of assault and battery, given that probable cause existed, the plaintiff would have to prove that the force used to detain the plaintiff had been excessive. Merchant detention statutes generally allow for "reasonable force" to detain persons suspected of shoplifting. A level of force beyond that which would be considered reasonable would place a store at risk. As long as probable cause exists and the level of force used to detain is reasonable, then a claim for assault and battery will undoubtedly fail.

Increasingly, stores are contracting outside security firms to provide the level of protection they deem necessary to maintain the stores' economic viability. What happens when a store hires a third party security service to police its premises? Can merchant protection statutes protect security firms' employees with the conditional privilege of apprehension and detention offered store employees? The answer sometimes is yes and sometimes is no. Some states' statutes specify that only merchants and their employees are protected. Other states' statutes specify that merchants, employees, and their agents are protected.

A case where the distinction became important occurred in Nebraska. In *Bishop v. Bockoven, Inc. and Metropolitan Protection Service, Inc.*, the wording of the state's merchant protection statute was specific as to whom it was intended to protect and to whom the conditional privilege of apprehension and detention applied.

As background, it was noted that Bishop was stopped by a security guard on leaving the Bockoven supermarket. The guard requested she return to the store. The guard escorted the plaintiff to the manager, where he explained that he saw plaintiff "double package" a pair of hosiery. Double packaging implies that an individual has placed an extra pair of hose in a package. The manager asked for and received permission to search two packages of hosiery that Bishop had purchased. Only one pair of hosiery was found in each package. The manager apologized, explained that a mistake had been made, and told

Bishop that she was free to leave. Subsequently, Bishop filed suit for damages related to her detention. The suit was filed against the store and Metropolitan Protection Service, Inc., an independent security contractor and the employer of the guard.

The district court dismissed the case against the store, citing the state's merchant detention statute and the actions of the store's employee. However, damages were awarded against Metropolitan. Metropolitan appealed, also claiming privilege under the state's merchant protection statute. The security firm argued that as an agent of the merchant, it was entitled to the benefits of the state's statute.

The Supreme Court of Nebraska affirmed the district court's finding that the security service was liable for false arrest and found that the state's statute was not applicable to security firms or other independent contractors working as agents for merchants. The Nebraska statute (NE ST § 29-402.1) is specific in its statement that "a peace officer, a merchant, or a merchant's employee" who has probable cause to believe that goods have been taken unlawfully from a merchant and that he or she can recover the goods by taking a person into custody may take the individual into custody and detain the individual without being rendered liable for slander, libel, false arrest, false imprisonment, or unlawful detention. The statute is clear that only peace officers, merchants, and their employees have the conditional privilege to detain suspects and garner civil liability protection.

The Supreme Court of Nebraska noted that the merchant protection statute grants a privilege to arrest or detain, and as such, it intrudes on a common-law right to be free from arrest or detention when no crime has been committed. The court noted that when statutes effect a change in common law or intrude on common-law rights, those statutes should be interpreted strictly. To develop a broad interpretation of an intrusive statute would not be in keeping with common law or the intent of the legislature.

When the wording of a statute is plain, direct, and unambiguous, as in the case of the merchant protection statute's delineation as to who is protected, no interpretation is needed to ascertain the intent of the legislature. The court will not interpret clear and specific language broadly. The court takes the point of view that had the legislature desired to broaden the classification of individuals the statute was designed to protect, it easily could have done so. A court cannot add words to a statute. In *Bishop*, the court concluded that the evidence was overwhelming in finding that the guard was not a peace officer, a merchant, nor a merchant's employee. Accordingly, the court found that the security firm was not privileged under the state's merchant protection statute and that liability had accrued to the guard service through the actions of the guard.

Bishop emphasizes an important point. Merchant protection statutes are specific. The individuals to whom protection is offered are delineated in the statutes. In the absence of a statutory privilege, a citizen is privileged to make an arrest only when a crime has been committed. If a crime has not been committed and a citizen makes an arrest without statutory privilege, liability will accrue.

To its dismay, Safeway Stores found that it was held responsible for the actions of a security guard provided it through an outside security agency. Despite the store's argument that the guard was not an employee and, as such, the store should not be held responsible for the guard's actions, the court found that the store could be held responsible for the actions of the guard.

In *Safeway Stores, Inc. v. Kelly*, Kelly sued for damages, charging that he had been falsely arrested and was the victim of an assault and battery. A chronology of incidents leading up to the filing of the suit may shed light on the charges. Kelly entered the Safeway store to shop for groceries. He noticed that the automatic door was not operating and required extra effort to open. According to his testimony, after he completed his shopping, he advised a cashier that he wanted to make a complaint about the broken door. Kelly was directed to the assistant manager, with whom he voiced his complaint. The assistant manager purportedly told Kelly that the door would be fixed within a few months and that he wished Kelly would stop making trouble for him. Kelly's testimony included a statement that he had not complained previously to the assistant manager. Kelly stated that the assistant manager told him he needed to leave the store or the assistant manager would have him arrested. Kelly indicated, though, that he had not realized that the employee's comments were ordering him to leave the store. Kelly allegedly responded that the store could call police, because he wanted to file a complaint. Kelly then went to the front of the store to await the police. The assistant manager was said to have called over the security guard who was on duty and directed another employee to call the police. Shortly thereafter, a police officer arrived. The officer spoke to the assistant manager. He then went to Kelly and informed him that the manager wanted him to leave the store.

Kelly's testimony indicated that before he could respond, the security guard came up behind him and grabbed him around his neck. At this time, the officer allegedly kneed Kelly in the chest, and then the officer and security guard pushed Kelly to the ground and handcuffed him. Kelly was taken to the back of the store and within minutes was transported to the police station, where he was charged with unlawful entry.

Testimony from others differed markedly from Kelly's in some respects. The officer said that upon entering the store, he heard loud shouting. Seeing the assistant manager and Kelly at the front of the store, he approached the assistant manager. The assistant manager told the officer that he had directed Kelly to leave, but Kelly had refused. The officer reported that he then approached Kelly and told him to leave. Kelly purportedly continued to shout, and the officer told him he was under arrest. The officer said Kelly raised his fist, but did not know if Kelly swung to hit him. The officer grabbed Kelly by the neck and pulled him to the ground. With the guard's help, the officer handcuffed Kelly, and they escorted him to the back of the store.

Three major considerations arose as a result of this case. First, was Kelly falsely arrested? Was he the victim of assault and battery by the security guard? If he was the victim of assault and battery by the security guard, was the store liable for that assault and battery?

The question as to the existence of probable cause as it relates to false arrest is a question of both law and fact. As is usual, when facts are in dispute, the question as to the existence of probable cause is for a jury to decide. But in instances where the facts are established or undisputed, the question becomes one of law, which must be addressed by the court.

In this case, Kelly was arrested by the police officer with assistance from the security guard. An individual who has no constitutional right or statutory right to remain on retail premises is guilty of unlawful entry if the individual refuses to leave when so ordered by the merchant. Testimony indicated that the assistant manager told Kelly to leave. The officer told Kelly to leave. Even Kelly's own testimony indicated that he was told to leave or face being arrested, though, amazingly, he said he had not understood that he was being directed to leave. Accordingly, the court found that probable cause existed to arrest Kelly for unlawful entry. The judgment against Safeway for false arrest was reversed.

The second area of concern is whether Kelly was the victim of assault and battery. Kelly testified that he offered no resistance. Despite this, his neck was grabbed from behind by the security guard and the guard pushed him to the ground, he alleged, although there was conflicting testimony. The court found that there was sufficient evidence upon which a jury could properly have found that Kelly had been the victim of an assault and battery.

The third area of concern, and one of direct importance to Safeway, is whether the store was liable for the actions of the guard. Safeway argued that the guard worked for a private security firm that was under contract to Safeway. As such, Safeway should not be held liable for the actions of another firm's employee. Testimony on behalf of Safeway indicated that the security firm hired, trained, paid, and directed the guards on how they were to perform their work. As per the contract,

Safeway paid a lump sum for all of guards supplied by the security firm. The chief security investigator for Safeway stated that the independent guards worked under the general direction of store managers. Managers had what was termed "operational control" over the guards. Managers set the hours guards worked, could replace guards deemed unsatisfactory, and could call on guards to assist in the handling of general security problems. Testimony by the guard generally paralleled that of Safeway's security chief. The guard testified that he would respond to specific requests for a variety of assistance matters, including the locking of doors at night. In addition, the guard testified that the security agency had trained him in the apprehension and arrest of shoplifters.

The question that begs to be asked is whether or not Safeway was responsible for the actions of the guard. If the guard was deemed independent, then Safeway was not likely to be found liable. If the guard, though, was considered a direct agent of the store, the store could have been held liable. Safeway argued that the guard was the employee of a private security firm, and thus the store was not liable for the guard's actions.

Unfortunately for Safeway, the District of Columbia Court of Appeals found that the store exercised sufficient control over the guard as to accrue liability related to wrongs committed by the guard on store premises. The court noted that the testimony indicated that managers had operational control over the guards. In short, the manager could set the guard's working hours, the manager could remove unsatisfactory guards, the manager could call on guards to lock doors in the evening, and the manager was free to call on the guards in a variety of situations where assistance was deemed necessary by the manager. As a result, the court found that there was sufficient evidence for a jury to have found that Safeway was liable for the assault and battery.

A few cases alleging damages from apprehensions and detentions related to shoplifting incidents have been heard in U.S. federal courts. Fewer still have named as a defendant the United States. The case of *Solomon v. United States* is among the latter. Pursued through the federal courts, Solomon's case sought recompense from the United States for damages allegedly incurred at the hands of security guards employed by a United States military base. In *Solomon*, the U.S. District Court for the Western District of Texas essentially found against the plaintiff when she brought suit for actions the security guards took following her exit from the military base's exchange (store). The purported damages were the result of what the plaintiff claimed was her false arrest and false imprisonment.

It was reported that upon exiting, two security guards employed by the base exchange stopped Solomon and asked that she accompany them back to the store. Once inside the store, Solomon's purse was searched. The guards found no shoplifted items among Solomon's belongings. Subsequently, Solomon filed suit in federal court claiming that the guards' actions, as "investigative or law enforcement officers" of the United States, placed the United States in the vicarious situation of being liable for their actions, which were purportedly without merit. As the investigative or law enforcement officers of the United States acted without regard to her rights, Solomon argued, the United States should not be able to claim sovereign immunity and instead should have to pay her for damages she sustained. Solomon's arguments centered around the fact that federal law now allows the United States to be held liable for certain unlawful actions of federal "investigative or law enforcement officers" acting in their capacity as investigative or law enforcement officers.

It should be noted that prior to 1974, sovereign immunity was a complete bar to legal action for civil damages filed against the United States for false arrests and false imprisonments initiated by government agents acting in their official capacity. However, in 1974 things changed. Federal law was changed. The Federal Tort Claims Act, 28 U.S.C. § 2680 (h), allowed the U.S. government to be held civilly liable where certain government agents were found to have committed specific intentional acts resulting in harm to others. The law specifically states that civil liability protection claimed under the auspices of sovereign immunity will *not* apply to

> any claim arising out of assault, battery, false imprisonment, false arrest, malicious prosecution, abuse of process, libel, slander, misrepresentation, deceit, or interference with contract rights: Provided that with regard to acts or omissions of investigative or law enforcement officers of the United States Government, the provisions of this chapter and section 1346(b) of this title shall apply to any claim arising, on or after the date of the enactment of this proviso, out of assault, battery, false imprisonment, false arrest, abuse of process, or malicious prosecution. For purpose of this subsection, "investigative or law enforcement officer" means any officer of the United States who is empowered by law to execute searches, to seize evidence, or to make arrests for violations of federal law.

In essence, the United States is allowing itself to be sued when any of the specific actions named above are committed by its "investigative or law enforcement officers."

As was seen in *Bishop v. Bockoven*, the courts are required to interpret laws as to their clear meaning. When the wording of a statute is clear and straightforward, a court will not creatively interpret the law so as to give credence to one argument or another. In instances where the wording of a law is not so clear, the court must, as is noted in the case, "construe the language so as to give effect to the intent of Congress." It will abide by the wording of the law as enacted or, in cases where the wording is unclear, will try to uphold the intent of Congress in an interpretation. In *Solomon*, the central question that begged to be answered was whether the 1974 changes to the federal code waived sovereign immunity and placed the United States at risk, given the circumstances of the case. The major issue to be resolved, then, was whether the security guards were "investigative or law enforcement officers" of the United States. If so, the claim of sovereign immunity would not stand, and the United States could be found liable for the actions of the guards. If the guards were not found to be "investigative or law enforcement officers" of the United States, then the United States (and its base exchange) would be protected under a claim of sovereign immunity.

The court noted that the changes in the law were predicated on the belief that individuals who had been wrongly harmed through false arrests, false imprisonments, and other specific acts should have the ability to seek recompense from the government. It was noted that the changes were in response to incidents where police raids were conducted at "wrong" addresses. Congress intended that sovereign immunity for false arrest and false imprisonment should be waived in limited circumstances. Specifically, the government stripped itself of a claim of sovereign immunity in cases in which investigative or law enforcement agents, acting within the scope of their federal employment or under color of federal law, committed false arrest, false imprisonment, slander, assault, and so forth.

For a security guard to be declared an "investigative or law enforcement officer," the guard would have to be empowered by federal law to execute searches, seize evidence, and make arrests for violations of federal law, and be acting within the scope of his or her employment when conducting such actions. The court noted that the security guards were not empowered to execute searches, seize evidence, nor make arrests for violations of federal law and that such actions, had they been conducted, would not have been within the scope of their employment.

As a result, the guards were not found to be investigative or law enforcement officers of the United States. As such, their efforts at the military base exchange did not remove the claim of sovereign immunity by the United States. The finding of the district court was affirmed by the United States Court of Appeals. The United States retains its right to claim sovereign immunity from torts committed on its military bases, except for specific torts committed by investigative or law enforcement officers empowered to make arrests for violations of federal law, conduct searches, and seize evidence pursuant to federal law. Again, while *Solomon* was a federal case involving sovereign immunity and not state merchant detention statutes, the finding is relevant: the wording of the statute and the intent of the legislative body enacting a law will be strictly interpreted and, when needed, interpreted with an eye to maintaining the intent of the legislature. The federal law, like state law, is specific as to what kinds of acts are covered, the individuals covered by the law, and the circumstances so covered.

In *Castaneda v. J. C. Penney, Inc.*, it was seen that the failure of a plaintiff to object during a trial as to the evidence presented as it related to the existence of probable cause to believe that shoplifting had been committed, whether a reasonable investigation had been conducted and for a reasonable period of time, and whether the investigation had been privileged under the state's merchant detention statute was not a reversible error on the part of the appellate court. In *Castaneda*, the plaintiff was stopped shortly after leaving a Penney's store, and an inquiry was conducted relative to some draperies. Eventually, Castaneda sued Penney's for illegal arrest, libelous slander, malicious prosecution, and false imprisonment. The trial court found for the store and Castaneda received nothing on her complaints.

Castaneda appealed claiming that the trial court erred in not requiring that all three issues as to reasonableness be addressed by defendants. The three issues, it was argued, centered around (1) whether there were reasonable grounds to believe that shoplifting had been committed, (2) whether the investigation had been conducted in a reasonable manner and in a reasonable period of time, and (3) whether the detention and investigation had been conducted for the purpose of investigating a shoplifting. On appeal, the Court of Civil Appeals of Texas affirmed the trial court's judgment, noting that the failure to submit these issues at the trial did not constitute grounds for a reversal, since the plaintiff had made no objection to the failure of the trial court to submit such issues.

Reasonableness must prevail. A detention must be based on probable cause, and an investigation must be conducted in a reasonable manner and for a reasonable period of time. Merchant protection statutes offer merchants protection, but it is a protection that is afforded only when actions are deemed reasonable and based on sufficient cause.

An interesting twist to the usual claim of protection under merchant detention statutes occurred in a case involving a casino and several individuals suspected of card counting. The case of *Bartolo v. Boardwalk Regency Hotel Casino, Inc.* witnessed a casino and its employees seeking protection from civil liability claims as charged by Bartolo and others. In this case, Bartolo, a brother, and two friends were allegedly falsely imprisoned as a result of their being detained and questioned by casino employees. The casino employees were acting on their belief that Bartolo and the others were counting cards in an effort to improve their chances at winning.

Testimony, which appeared to be largely uncontested, indicated that the four men had previously lost money gambling at the casino. They later returned, and while playing blackjack, were approached by two uniformed guards, who indicated that they believed that the four had been counting cards and asked that they accompany them to the games manager. Allegedly, one of the guards grasped one of the men by the collar, and the men were taken away from the table so quickly that they had not removed all of their chips from play. The four were escorted by the guards to the games manager, who asked for their identification. He indicated that the four would not be allowed to gamble at the casino in the future due to their counting cards. The four initially refused to supply their identification to the manager, who then threatened to have them arrested. The four claimed they had not been counting cards but did supply their identifications to the manager. The names were entered on a pad the manager kept, and he told the four that they would not be allowed to play at the Boardwalk or at other casinos as a result of their actions. Bartolo and the others were then told to leave the casino.

After the plaintiffs reportedly tried to lodge a formal complaint with the state's casino control commission, they met with the casino's assistant manager, who purportedly apologized to the men, offered to buy them a meal, and indicated that they could play blackjack in the casino. However, Bartolo and the others were not appeased by this offer and subsequently filed suit, claiming they were falsely imprisoned, slandered, and assaulted. The case here revolved around the claim of false imprisonment and, specifically, the fact that the casino sought summary judgment to have the suit dismissed. Claiming immunity similar to that afforded merchants apprehending and detaining shoplifters, the casino took the position that it should have been protected, since its employees were acting on probable cause and in good faith. New Jersey has a specific law, similar to that offered retail merchants, that affords casinos a privilege to detain when probable cause exists to believe an individual is cheating or using devices that aid their ability to cheat casinos. The points central to the case are whether or not casinos have the right to detain individuals suspected of counting cards and whether such action is privileged under New Jersey's law.

False imprisonment is a serious concern. It is evidenced by a restraint of one's freedom that is clearly unlawful. Such an unlawful restraint on one's freedom can be effectuated by a physical force or by a threat of force. The use of physical force to restrain an individual is easy to show and seldom brought into question. What is less obvious, but can still form the basis of a restraint, is the force that can be brought to bear by words or conduct that carry the meaning of force. The courts have long taken the point of view that if a person feels reasonably unable to go about business as usual due to the belief that he or she is being held by some force, even a force that is not physical in nature, then that person is being denied his or her liberty. In other words, when a person asserts he or she has the legal power to make another go somewhere, as is sometimes the case with security personnel showing a badge, grabbing an individual's arm, and directing that individual back into a retail store, then individuals who are responding to such a statement may feel justified in thinking they are being detained. Such a showing of force (the badge and orders to return) is often the basis for an individual's feeling forced to return to a store, and if the detention is shown to have been without cause, the unlawful use of force will be seen as false imprisonment.

In *Bartolo*, the casino contended that its employees had the right to detain individuals they suspected of card counting and thus argued that its employees acted lawfully when they temporarily detained the plaintiffs. For the uninitiated, card counting is a process in which players keep track of the value of cards played and, as a result, place larger bets when the odds are shown to favor the player rather than the house. Good counters are said to be able to significantly alter the expected payout by taking into account the statistical probabilities associated with playing cards and increasing their bets when the odds favor the player. Thus card counting involves nothing more than using known mathematical or statistical probabilities as an aid in betting. It does not involve cheating or the use of any physical device to hide or alter cards. It can be argued that card counters are mathematically astute, as card counting, especially when multiple decks are dealt, is a difficult practice at best, and impossible for many. It should be noted that card counting, as normally practiced, is not against the law; nor does it involve any kind of dishonesty.

It should be noted that the state's casino control commission allowed casinos to reject card counters, basing its stand on state law, which allows a proprietor to exclude a patron from business premises for any reason. However, as was noted, such a stand was overturned by an appellate court, and was in the process of being reviewed by the state's supreme court.

The court in *Bartolo* distinguished between the right of a proprietor to deny entry to a person due to dishonest acts (shoplifting) and honest acts (card counting). Merchants are allowed a privilege to detain persons they suspect and have cause to suspect are shoplifting. This privilege is granted to merchants who possess probable cause with the distinct understanding that its purpose is to effect recovery of merchandise that is believed to have been stolen. Further, the privilege is granted with protection from civil damages, provided that detentions are based on probable cause, conducted in a reasonable manner, and concluded in a reasonable period of time. It is important to note that merchant protection statutes cover merchants who are conducting investigations of acts of shoplifting, acts that by definition are blatantly illegal. *Bartolo*, on the other hand, concerned actions that are legal.

The casino proffered that its employees enjoyed an immunity similar to that offered retail merchants. New Jersey has a state law that applies to casino operators; it offers a conditional privilege of detention similar to that which retail merchants enjoy. However, that law provides that casino employees who possess probable cause for believing that individuals are in the process of trying to cheat a casino (through a variety of enumerated, specific practices) may take such persons into custody, in a reasonable manner and for a reasonable length of time, for the purpose of notifying authorities. The statute further provides that such a detention shall not render the employee or the casino civilly liable for false arrest, slander, or unlawful detention. To those in retailing, these words are familiar. The casino must possess probable cause to believe an illegal act is taking or took place, that it is being cheated or was cheated. A detention must be conducted in a reasonable manner and concluded in a reasonable period of time. Given these three factors, casino operators are protected.

The current case though, involved no illegality. The court noted that the plaintiffs were not cheating the casino. They were not using any device or sleight-of-hand tricks to cheat the casino out of its property or money. The plaintiffs were accused of counting cards, an act that, if it occurred, was a legal act at the time this case arose. The attempt by the casino to get a summary judgment granted in its favor was denied. The court noted that absent any statutory authority to detain card counters, the plaintiff's version of the incident at the casino would constitute false imprisonment, and as such, a summary judgment in favor of the defendants could not ensue.

The privilege to detain individuals suspected of shoplifting carries with it a major responsibility. Merchants may detain suspected shoplifters only when they have probable cause to do so. The detention must be conducted in a reasonable manner and concluded in a reasonable period of time. Merchants and their employees who move to detain individuals will place themselves at risk should they not have probable cause for their actions.

Table 4.1
Citations and Management Implications in Chapter Four

Case	Implication
Mahon v. King's Department Store, Inc., 25 ATLA L.Rep. 31	Merchant detention statutes allow searches of handbags, shopping bags, and other items. Searching within a suspect's clothing or undressing a suspect may place a merchant at risk. A merchant is not privileged to undress or to order the undressing of suspects. Actions that are not reasonable will be seen as unlawful.
Bryant v. Sears, Roebuck & Company, 25 ATLA L.Rep. 271	The merchant's privilege does not extend to the searching inside of a suspect's clothing or the undressing of suspects.
City Stores Company v. Gibson, 263 A.2d 252 (D.C.App. 1970)	Merchant protection statutes do not empower merchants to disrobe or to order the disrobing of suspects. Suspects may recover damages for humiliation.
Cervantez v. J. C. Penney Company, Inc., 595 P.2d 975 (Cal. 1979)	Different levels of cause are required of a police officer and a citizen (merchant) in order to make an arrest in a shoplifting incident. The crime must be committed in the presence of a citizen in order for the citizen to effect an arrest.
Wilson v. Wal-Mart Stores, Inc., 525 So.2d 11 (La.App. 3Cir. 1988)	Reasonable cause for investigatory purposes is viewed as something less than probable cause. Merchant protection statutes exist so that merchants can conduct business without fear regarding actions taken in good faith.
Coblyn v. Kennedy's, Inc., 268 N.E.2d 860 (Mass. 1971)	Reasonableness must be at the basis of store employee actions. Lacking reasonableness and failing to establish probable cause will leave a store vulnerable.
Mapes v. National Food Stores of Louisiana, Inc., 329 So.2d 831 (La.App. 1Cir. 1976)	Investigations must be reasonable to be lawful. Probable cause is at the center of reasonableness.

Table 4.1 (*Continued*)

Case	Implication
Rusnak v. Giant Foods, Inc., 337 A.2d 445 (Md.S.App. 1975)	Stores are not responsible for the actions of off-duty employees acting as private citizens. When off-duty employees are on the premises and acting as private citizens, the off-duty employees may accrue liability for actions that are deemed unlawful.
Montgomery Ward & Company, Inc. v. Keulemans, 340 A.2d 705 (Md.App. 1975)	Lacking probable cause, a detention becomes unlawful. An unlawful detention that is seen as malicious may result in the awarding of punitive damages.
Gabrou v. May Department Stores Company, 462 A.2d 1102 (D.C.App. 1983)	An assault and battery may be found to occur if the force used to detain an individual is seen as excessive. State statutes generally allow the use of "reasonable force" to detain persons suspected of shoplifting.
Johnson v. Bloomingdale's, 420 N.Y.S.2d 840 (N.Y.S. 1979)	New York's statute does not authorize fingerprinting or photographing of suspects by merchants. Fingerprinting and photographing shoplifting suspects may make a detention unreasonable and leave a store vulnerable to civil damages.
Bishop v. Bockoven, Inc., and Metropolitan Protection Service, Inc., 260 N.W.2d 488 (Neb. 1977)	Statutes are specific regarding to whom protection is offered. Courts will not creatively interpret wording that is clear and unambiguous.
Safeway Stores, Inc. v. Kelly, 448 A.2d 856 (D.C.App. 1982)	A store may be held liable for the actions of guards obtained through outside security firms.
Lerner Shops of Nevada, Inc. v. J. P. Marin, 423 P.2d 398 (Nev. 1967)	Submission to the verbal direction of another, unaccompanied by force or threats of force, does not constitute false imprisonment.
Black v. Clark's Greensboro, Inc., 139 S.E.2d 199 (N.C. 1964)	False imprisonment is construed as a restraint of an individual's liberty without sufficient cause.

(Continued)

Table 4.1 (*Continued*)

Case	Implication
Hales v. McCrory-McLellan Corporation, 133 S.E.2d 225 (N.C. 1963)	Having a police officer assist in an unlawful restraint does nothing to legitimize the restraint. An unlawful restraint is unlawful regardless of who is involved in the restraint.
Martinez v. Goodyear Tire & Rubber Company, 651 S.W.2d 18 (Tex.App. 4Dist. 1983)	A person who has reasonable cause to believe another has stolen or is attempting to steal retail property is privileged to detain the person in a reasonable manner for a reasonable period of time for investigating ownership of the property.
Solomon v. United States, 559 F.2d 309 (5th Cir. 1977)	Claims of sovereign immunity may be waived in the event that federal law enforcement agents commit specific torts, such as false arrests and false imprisonments, while in the conduct of their federal law enforcement duties. Security guards working at military base exchanges are not law enforcement agents.
Castaneda v. J. C. Penney, Inc., 438 S.W.2d 938 (Tex.App. 1969)	Reasonableness depends on probable cause and a reasonable investigation conducted in a reasonable time period. Failure to object to major issues in a trial will not be sufficient reason to reverse a lower court ruling.
Bartolo v. Boardwalk Regency Hotel Casino, Inc., 449 A.2d 1339 (N.J.Super.L. 1982)	To garner protection of merchant protection statutes, merchants must suspect that an individual has committed a criminal act (shoplifting).

SUMMARY OF CONCEPTS IN CHAPTER FOUR

1. An unrestrained use of force can result in a loss of civil liability immunity. Merchant detention statutes allow reasonable force to be used to detain persons for whom probable cause exists to believe that the persons are in the act of shoplifting or have shoplifted.

2. Undressing a suspect or ordering a suspect to undress is not privileged under the law. Such an unlawful action will expose the merchant to civil liability.

3. Differences in some states' statutes allow for different levels of cause to detain depending on whether one is a merchant or a police officer. For example, in California, a police officer may make an arrest on the basis of probable cause, while a merchant may initiate a detention only when a crime is committed in the presence of the merchant.

4. It is important to maintain constant surveillance of shoplifting suspects.

5. Apprehension and detention must be conducted in a reasonable manner. Lacking reasonableness, a detention may be considered unlawful.

6. Probable cause or sufficient cause and reasonableness must be at the center of a detention to ensure civil liability immunity.

7. False imprisonment is a serious restraint of a person's liberty without sufficient cause. It is assumed that an individual who has been falsely imprisoned has been harmed, and damages will ensue.

8. An individual who voluntarily allows him- or herself to be detained in order to establish innocence will find it difficult to establish that a false imprisonment has occurred.

9. Normally, a store will not be liable for the off-duty actions of employees, even when the actions in question occur in the store, when employees are acting on their own and not as agents of the store.

10. Punitive damages can be awarded only when, in the absence of probable cause, malice is shown to exist or can be implied.

11. Merchant protection statutes are specific regarding whom is offered civil liability immunity. In some states, guards from an outside agency working under contract for a store may not enjoy civil liability immunity.

Chapter Five

Shoplifting Detention Duration Concerns

Merchant detention statutes all state that such detention should be no longer than a certain period of time (usually stated as one hour or sixty minutes) or be only for a reasonable length of time. Managers and their employees need to be aware of this area of concern and proceed accordingly. Those who fail to comply with this aspect of their state's statute will leave themselves vulnerable.

In two related cases that were consolidated for trial, the case of *Schmidt v. Richman Gordman, Inc. and Horan* and the case of *Clifton v. Richman Gordman, Inc. and Horan,* two sisters successfully argued that they were detained beyond the limits allowed in Nebraska's merchant detention statutes. Specifically, the sisters leveled a variety of charges, including false imprisonment and detention beyond a reasonable length of time. The sisters' suits also accused the store of malicious prosecution.

According to the record, the two were stopped by a store security guard (Horan) as they were leaving the store with younger family members. The guard had reportedly observed the sisters as they were shopping. The two had picked out a shirt and vest and, placing them together on a hanger, appeared to proceed and then try to match a tie to the ensemble. Not finding a suitable tie, the sisters proceeded to pick out a pair of gloves to go with the shirt and vest. Meanwhile, Horan, believing that the women intended to steal the shirt, advised the checkout clerk that she should give the women an opportunity to pay for the shirt and arranged for the clerk to give a signal should they pay only for the vest. While checking them out, the clerk inquired of the sisters as to whether the shirt and vest on the hanger were a "one-piece item" or a "two-piece item." Both sisters reported that they responded it was "two pieces." Further, they reported that the clerk separated the two items and that price tags were clearly visible on both pieces. The clerk bagged the merchandise, stapled the receipt to it, and, as the women left, signaled Horan.

Horan quickly approached the women, showed them her badge, and requested that they accompany her to the office. Once there, the sisters gave Horan permission to check the contents of the bag. Schmidt testified that Horan told them they had not paid for the shirt. One of the sisters replied that they had just gone through the checkout and paid for everything. Horan displayed the receipt, which did not indicate a payment for the shirt. The sisters said that they had intended to pay for the shirt and that if they had not, it was not their fault but the clerk's.

Insisting that the two sisters intended to shoplift the shirt, the store's security guard proceeded to notify authorities. The plaintiffs were held in the store for approximately forty-five minutes. Police officers summoned to the store were advised that the two had been shoplifting in the store. The sisters were transported to the police station, where they were fingerprinted, photographed, booked, and released on bail. It was reported that the sisters spent between three and four hours in police custody. Subsequently, their criminal cases were dismissed and they filed suit claiming they were falsely imprisoned (without cause, in an unreasonable manner, and for an unreasonable length of time) and that the prosecution was malicious.

At trial, the clerk testified that the store normally used both a color code and a written code on two-piece items to indicate that there was to be only a single charge for the two pieces. The clerk testified that she only saw one price tag and could not remember whether or not she had separated the items; nor could she remember whether or not the items were coded as a multiple-piece item. Further, the clerk confirmed that at least one of the sisters, when asked at the register, had responded that the shirt and vest were "two pieces." The clerk reportedly made no attempt to eliminate any possible misunderstanding between her and the sisters concerning whether or not it was a one-piece item or a two-piece item.

The lower court held that the length of time the sisters were detained was unreasonable and awarded the sisters damages for false arrest and imprisonment and for malicious prosecution. The ruling that the length of time the sisters were detained was an unreasonable length of time was upheld by the appellate court, and, while the amount of damages awarded was slightly decreased due to the fact that the jury had awarded more to the plaintiffs than was sought, the incident deserves a closer look.

In looking at some of the specific concerns that arose in the appeal, two overriding concerns should be pointed out. First, when the sisters were in the store office, were they falsely imprisoned? Second, since the charge of malicious prosecution resulted in the largest portion of the damages awarded the plaintiffs, what is meant by malicious prosecution?

False imprisonment is a serious offense. As was stated by the appellate court, "False imprisonment consists in the unlawful restraint against his will of an individual's liberty." Any conduct that prevents an individual from going where one may lawfully go may constitute false imprisonment. In this case, the sisters testified that when they were in the store's security office, they felt they could not leave. At the same time, Horan indicated that should the plaintiffs have run from the office, she would have given chase. This type of situation, where individuals feel constrained, where they believe they are unable to leave, may result in charges of false imprisonment. The fact that the security guard indicated that she would have given chase adds further to the notion that the two sisters were being restrained.

Malicious prosecution is a serious affair. It is evident, too, that enlisting the aid or assistance of law enforcement in the process does not relieve the original complainant of liability for such actions. To qualify as a malicious prosecution, the following six factors must be present.

1. A legal proceeding must have been commenced against the plaintiff.
2. The legal proceeding must have been caused or effected by the defendant.
3. The termination of the proceeding must have been in favor of the plaintiff.
4. The plaintiff must show an absence of probable cause as a basis for commencing the proceeding.
5. The presence of malice on the part of the defendants must exist.
6. The presence of damages resulting from the prosecution must exist.

Should a plaintiff be able to show that these six factors were present in his or her prosecution, then that plaintiff will prevail on a malicious prosecution charge. All six factors must be present, or the finding of malicious prosecution will not ensue. In the present case, store employees' actions did result in the restraint and prosecution of the plaintiffs. The appellate court noted that the city prosecutor's actions were based on the report furnished by the defendants and that the defendants failed to give the city prosecutor all information relating to the cases (primarily this referred to the store not relaying to the prosecutor the sisters' version of what happened). The cases against the sisters were dismissed in their favor. The existence of probable cause was disputed by the parties, but the court noted that the jury's finding against the defendants reflected their finding that probable cause did not exist. In looking to see whether malice is present in a prosecution, a variety of factors may come into play. The law does not assume malice exists. It must be shown to exist or it may be inferred to exist by actions not based on probable cause. The mere lack of probable cause, though, does not in itself indicate the existence of malice. A jury may, as in this case, after reviewing all of the evidence, draw the conclusion that malice was present based on the actions of individuals, who despite lacking probable cause, proceeded with their complaints. Finally, the plaintiffs were able to show that they had been damaged. Their liberty was restrained. They were booked into jail, fingerprinted, and photographed. The plaintiffs incurred direct legal costs associated with hiring attorneys for their defense. Basically, the six factors to determine malicious prosecution were present, and the finding of the jury that such maliciousness did exist was reason to award damages for malicious prosecution.

The finding for the two sisters by the trial court and the verdict's affirmation by the appellate court serves notice to merchants as to the importance of possessing probable cause when pursuing a prosecution. The miscommunication between the clerk and the customers and a host of other factors led to an embarrassment for the store, unhappy customers, and bad publicity. It is important to ascertain all of the facts quickly and to base a decision as to whether to prosecute on all of the facts.

It can be argued that a detention not based on probable cause is too long a detention regardless of length. And in general, such a detention is by definition unreasonably long. Because of this, most suits by individuals against stores for false arrest or illegal detention have as their core the charge that the detention is unreasonably long. As such, most suits don't specifically include a charge of unreasonable length, since an unreasonable detention encompasses the concept of an unreasonable duration as to the length of the detention.

Louisiana's merchant detention statute stipulates that detentions related to the investigation of retail thefts are not to take longer than one hour. Store employees in Louisiana who apprehend and detain individuals they suspect of retail theft need to be cognizant of the need to complete their efforts within the one-hour limit as allowed by law. To emphasize the point, a suit was filed in Louisiana seeking $100,000 against a store and its manager by a person who charged that she had been illegally detained in the store by the store's employees for two hours (Budden, Miller, Yeargain, and Culverhouse, 1991).

Stores need to have policies and procedures that delineate which actions store employees should follow. Store employees need to act professionally when apprehending and detaining individuals they suspect of retail theft. Employees need to act courteously whenever possible. Employees need to act pursuant to their store policies. Store policies need to be established that would cover expectations as to employee actions as they pertain to detentions. Store policy expectations need to parallel expectations of state merchant protection or detention statutes. And finally, store employees need to know, understand, and follow sound policies and procedures as they relate to apprehensions and detentions.

In a case tried in Arkansas, *Wal-Mart Stores, Inc. v. Yarbrough*, an employee of the store observed Yarbrough placing a pen on or partially in her purse. The employee quickly notified the store's assistant manager. The assistant manager then began observing Yarbrough. He observed her for approximately ten minutes. Yarbrough exited through the checkout counter, paying for several items. The pen, still visible in the purse, was not placed with the other items to be checked out. Once she was outside the store, the assistant manager approached Yarbrough and asked if she had paid for the pen. She replied that she had forgotten the pen was in her purse and would return to the cashier to pay for it.

The assistant manager and another employee accompanied Yarbrough into the store. Yarbrough was steered clear of the checkout counter and directed to the rear of the store, where she was accompanied by two employees. Testimony indicated that the employees were there to prevent a possible escape. The police were called, and the assistant manager notified Yarbrough that she was under arrest. Yarbrough continued to insist that she had just forgotten to pay for the pen and that she was willing to do so.

Testimony indicated that Wal-Mart had established a procedure for detaining, interrogating, and prosecuting shoplifting suspects. The procedure required interrogation after a detention. The store policy allowed managers the freedom to decide that a suspect simply forgot to pay for a purchase and, correspondingly, allowed managers the latitude to release individuals after such a determination. Such a determination was to be based on the personal observation of the suspect and the results of the interrogation. Further, the written procedure stated specifically that just because an item was not paid for did not necessarily mean a person was guilty of shoplifting. The assistant manager later testified that he was not familiar with the store's procedures for handling shoplifting suspects.

After hearing Yarbrough's version of the events leading to her arrest, the prosecutor recommended to Wal-Mart that the charge be dismissed. Wal-Mart's management insisted that once the arrest had been made, the store would prosecute. Yarbrough was tried and, perhaps not surprisingly, was acquitted.

Yarbrough sued Wal-Mart for false arrest, false imprisonment, malicious prosecution, and intentional infliction of emotional distress. Wal-Mart moved for summary judgments and directed verdicts on all issues. The trial court dismissed the issues of false arrest and intentional infliction of emotional distress. However, the motions on the other charges were denied.

The jury awarded Yarbrough compensatory damages. It also awarded her $20,000 in punitive damages. On appeal, these awards were upheld. The Arkansas Supreme Court upheld the award of damages and cited the assistant manager's conscious indifference to the consequences of his actions. The court seemed particularly concerned that no effort had been made to listen to or to believe Yarbrough's explanation and that the prosecutor's recommendation to drop the charges had been ignored.

Based on the findings of this case, it is apparent that a detention and an arrest of an individual must be conducted in a justifiable and legal manner. When the specifics of the law and of a store's sound procedures are unknown or disregarded by a merchant, the store becomes vulnerable to damaging suits and to a loss of credibility. Stores need to have sound procedures that are based on the law, and their employees need to know and follow those procedures.

Weissman v. K-Mart Corporation resulted in conclusions similar to that drawn from *Yarbrough*. In *Weissman*, testimony indicated that the store's security officer observed Weissman holding an unstapled bag in the store and attaching a colored piece of paper to the bag with a rubber band. The store used colored papers to distinguish bags that had been carried into the store from the outside and bags containing store merchandise paid for by customers desiring to return to the store to continue shopping. Typically, the papers were stapled to the bags by store employees situated at the front of the store.

Weissman was approached by the security guard and questioned about the bag and its contents. Weissman could not find the receipt for the items in the bag and asked that the security guard allow a clerk to verify that he had paid for the items. The request to have a clerk verify the purchases was refused. The police were summoned, arrived quickly, and took Weissman into custody. Weissman was detained in the store less than thirty minutes.

At Weissman's trial, the cashier who had waited on Weissman appeared on his behalf. The store's security guard who had initiated the detention failed to appear. The case was discharged for lack of prosecution. Subsequently, Weissman filed suit for false arrest, malicious prosecution, slander, and intentional infliction of emotional distress.

The trial court granted summary judgment for K-Mart and its security employees. On appeal, the appellate court noted that Florida's merchant detention statute protects merchants, their employees, and peace officers from civil liability when probable cause to detain suspected shoplifters is shown to have existed. The court found, however, that due to the conflicting testimony between Weissman and K-Mart security employees, the determination as to the existence of probable cause should have gone to the jury. The jury should have determined whether the guard acted reasonably and with probable cause. The determination as to whether or not the security guard should have spoken to the cashier before initiating an arrest should have been decided by the jury. The court cited a rule from *City of Pensacola v. Owens* that where it would appear to a prudent man that further investigation is justified before instituting proceedings, liability may attach for failure to do so. The court was quite clearly unhappy with the security officer's unwillingness to speak to the cashier.

That the security employee initially had probable cause to detain Weissman appears to have been the case. However, not approaching the cashier and having her confirm or deny payment was a mistake. A store must legally detain suspects, and such a detention requires reasonableness. Such a detention requires probable cause. Once probable cause ceases to exist, then the privilege to detain ceases to exist. Some may argue that courtesy required that the guard at least have asked the cashier to confirm whether or not a purchase had been made. Lacking such a courtesy, the store found the trial court's summary judgment reversed and itself facing a trial for damages.

It is important to note that a detention of relatively short duration, one that is well within the scope of what ordinarily may be termed a reasonable length of time, for instance, the time necessary to wait for an order while in line at the drive-in window of a fast food restaurant, may not qualify as a reasonable amount of time to detain someone for investigatory purposes if probable cause to detain the person does not exist. In a case in which testimony indicated that a detention lasted less than five minutes, a store was found liable for the detention when probable cause was found not to have existed.

In *West v. Wal-Mart Stores, Inc.*, the detention, which lasted less than five minutes, was deemed unreasonable given the circumstances. Reasonableness as it relates to cause is a necessity when determining whether or not to apprehend a suspected shoplifter. In *West*, the store's support team manager, who was assigned to watch for shoplifters, noticed customers (the Wests) leaving the cashier area at the front of the store with a cart full of checked goods. At the same time, he noted a large bag of dog food on the shelf at the bottom of the cart. Believing that the cashier had failed to charge the couple for the dog food, the manager caught up with the couple as they were exiting the store. He then asked to see their cash register receipt and indicated he thought they may have failed to pay for the dog food.

The Wests stated that they had paid for the dog food and showed the manager their receipt. Due to the cash register's light print, the manner in which the receipt had been stapled to the bag, and a smear on the receipt itself, the manager could not discern the dog food listing, which, as it turned out, was the first item on the list. Since he could not make out the charge for the dog food, he asked the Wests to return to the inside of the store. Once they were there, he asked in a loud voice, it was reported, whether the couple had been charged for the dog food. The question was directed at the cashier the manager thought had checked out the couple. The cashier responded that she had not checked out that couple. Another cashier nearby confirmed that she had checked out the Wests and that they had paid for the dog food. The manager apologized to the Wests and thanked them for shopping at the store.

Mrs. West became incensed and started crying. The Wests then asked to see both the customer service manager and the store's general manager to complain. The managers apologized for the incident and for any embarrassment caused by the support team manager's actions. The Wests left the store and subsequently filed suit against the store.

Again, the testimony indicated that the detention took less than five minutes. The Wests stayed in the store approximately thirty-five additional minutes filing their complaints with the managers. The court ruled in favor of the Wests, finding that Wal-Mart's employee had no reasonable cause to detain the couple because the support manager had observed no furtive appearance or suspicious conduct on the part of the Wests. Apparently, the support manager had not observed them at the checkout counter; he did not know which cashier had checked them out. The support manager had not bothered to question any cashier before the detention to ascertain whether or not he should be concerned about the dog food's placement on the bottom shelf of the basket. Additionally, there was nothing unusual about the position of the dog food in the cart, and it admittedly was customary to place large bags of dog food in the carts without additional store bagging.

On appeal, the decision for West was amended (the award was reduced), but the finding that the support manager lacked reasonable cause to detain West was affirmed. Even a short detention, one of only a few minutes, can leave a store vulnerable when it is without probable cause. State statutes generally allow a privileged detention for a reasonable period of time. Lacking sufficient cause, any detention, regardless of duration, will undoubtedly be construed to be unreasonable.

A necklace placed inside a mug and not paid for led to charges being filed against a customer and eventually a suit against the store. In the case of *Gibson's Products, Inc. v. Edwards*, Edwards and her witnesses testified that she was shopping in Gibson's with her children. She reported that among the many items she selected and placed in her basket were a mug and a necklace. Edwards testified that her children also carried items to the front. Once at the register, Edwards reported that she placed the items on the counter to be rung up. Her children distracted her while the cashier was busy totaling the purchase. The necklace had been placed in a mug that was among the items. After paying the bill, Edwards left the store. She was then approached by a store employee, who asked about the necklace. After responding that she had paid for her purchases, she was asked to return to the store, which she did. Once she was in the store, Edwards's bag was emptied. The necklace, which had not been rung up, was retrieved. Police were called, and she was taken into custody.

The testimony of store employees was in almost total disagreement with that of Edwards and her witnesses. The store employee who initiated the apprehension (Fitzpatrick) reported seeing Edwards conceal a necklace in her hand. He followed her around the store as she shopped. He testified that at the counter, Edwards placed the necklace in the mug and displayed the mug to the cashier in a manner that allowed the cashier to note the mug's price but not reveal its contents. Further, he stated that she had only two items in the bag, the mug and the necklace. The cashier's testimony was less certain. The cashier reported seeing no children with Edwards but indicated that they may have been at the gum machines in front of the store. Fitzpatrick and an off-duty police officer working as a guard reported seeing the children standing beside Edwards in line.

After her arrest, Edwards posted bond and was released. The warrant for her arrest was later dismissed. Shortly thereafter, Edwards filed suit against Gibson's, seeking damages for false arrest and malicious prosecution. The jury found for Edwards and awarded her both compensatory and punitive damages. Gibson's appealed and argued that its employees acted reasonably and on the basis of probable cause. The state's (Georgia's) merchant detention statute allows that there should be no civil recovery for false arrest or false imprisonment arising out of a detention or arrest when the behavior of an individual gives one probable cause to believe that the individual is shoplifting.

The Court of Appeals of Georgia concluded that since the evidence submitted was in such dispute, the trial court had been correct in submitting the question of probable cause to the jury. The determination as to the existence of probable cause by the jury led to the finding in favor of Edwards. Further, the appellate court ruled that the instructions related to punitive damages directed to the jury had been proper. As a result, the appellate court affirmed the lower court's judgment awarding compensatory and punitive damages to the plaintiff.

Store employees and managers need to recognize that state merchant protection statutes have been enacted with the purpose of providing protection to store employees who are acting lawfully to protect their property interests. Lawful actions are those that are reasonable and based on the possession of sufficient cause to believe that a crime has been committed or is being committed. Lacking sufficient cause, detentions are not privileged and stores are vulnerable. As was seen in a California case, *People v. Lee*, the court held that a "private citizen may arrest another when circumstances exist which would cause a reasonable person to believe that a crime had been committed." Store procedures and the actions of store employees need to have as a central tenet the concept of reasonableness.

A case with implications similar to those in *West* involved a drugstore located in Mississippi. In that case, *Southwest Drug Stores of Mississippi, Inc. v. Garner*, it was seen that an employee should have investigated further before initiating a detention involving the alleged theft of a bar of soap.

Testimony indicated that Garner and her sister had gone to the drugstore to make some purchases. Their ill father, who reportedly was hard of hearing, remained in the car parked in front of the store while his daughters entered the store to shop. Upon entering, Garner went to the cosmetic counter to look at soap. The store manager asked if he might help, and when Garner replied that she wanted some soap, the store manager directed a female employee to assist Garner. With the assistance of the salesclerk, Garner found the soap she was looking for and, accompanied by the clerk, went to the cashier to pay for it. She received her receipt and the soap, which was placed in a small bag.

Garner's sister continued to shop while Garner left the store to check on her father. As she walked to her car in the parking lot, the store manager ran after her, calling in a loud voice for her to stop. Garner testified that the manager loudly accused her of stealing a bar of soap. She asked the store manager if he meant the soap in the bag, and he replied yes. She said he continued to accuse her of stealing the soap and directed her back into the store to prove it. Garner said a number of people were close by and heard the manager's accusation. The manager did not grab Garner; nor at any time did he hold her in any manner. Once in the store, the cashier confirmed Garner's statement that she had paid for the soap. Reportedly embarrassed, Garner began crying. The manager apologized and allowed her to leave. Garner reported that the incident made her sick and that she made two visits to a doctor as a result. Garner's father testified that he heard the manager yell at his daughter to stop but that due to poor hearing, he could not hear the details of the conversation between his daughter and the manager.

The specific event leading to the detention, according to the manager, was his seeing Garner put a bar of soap in her bag and walk out. The manager asked the cashier if Garner had paid for a particular brand name of soap, to which the cashier said no. He then went to detain Garner. The manager denied that he accused Garner of stealing the soap and said that when he saw it was not the brand of soap he thought it to be, he apologized, and reported that Garner herself insisted that they return to the store.

At trial, the jury decided that the store manager had lacked sufficient cause to believe that a crime had been committed and that as such the detention was not privileged. A sizable award for damages was awarded by the jury. The store argued that the manager had acted reasonably, that he had had sufficient cause to believe that a crime was being committed, and that the detention was reasonable. The store appealed the award.

The store's appeal centered on the fact that the detention should have been determined to be privileged under Mississippi's law (MS ST § 97-23-95), which says in part that a "merchant or any employee thereof or any peace or police officer, acting in good faith and upon probable cause based upon reasonable grounds therefor, may question such person, in a reasonable manner for the purpose of ascertaining whether or not such person is guilty of shoplifting as defined herein. Such questioning of a person by a merchant, merchant's employee, or peace or police officer shall not render such merchant, merchant's employee or peace or police officer civilly liable for slander, false arrest, false imprisonment, malicious prosecution, unlawful detention." The store's argument that the manager possessed probable cause and had acted reasonably was at the center of its appeal. Relative to the charge of slander, the store argued that any comments the manager made were reasonable and as such were privileged under the merchant protection statute.

Although it can be argued that qualified privilege may have existed, the privilege was lost by the manner in which the detention was perceived to have been conducted. In other words, the jury found that the manager's loud voice and rude accusation of stealing, delivered in such a way that others outside the store could hear, were unreasonable. The court noted that the manager may have had reason to detain Garner after seeing her place the soap in her purse but that the manner of the investigation left little doubt in the minds of the jury that it had not been conducted in a reasonable manner.

The appellate court concluded that the trial court's finding of fault on the part of the store manager and the award of damages were correct. The conflicting testimony concerning the existence of probable cause mandated a jury decision. The size of the award, while arguably large, was not deemed to be unduly large or to be a product of bias or prejudice on the part of the jury. As a result, the findings and the award of the lower court were affirmed.

Again, lacking probable cause, any duration of a detention may be deemed to be too long. If a detention is seen as unreasonable by a jury, the duration, regardless of how short, may be deemed to be too long. Store employees must have probable cause to detain an individual for investigatory purposes. Store employees conducting a detention must do so in a reasonable manner and for a reasonable length of time.

It is interesting to note that merchant detention statutes are just that, statutes that protect retail merchants. All of the states' merchant protection statutes, while sometimes extending the offer of privileged apprehension and detention to others, as in the case of California's law, which, as was seen, is applicable to theater owners and librarians, were developed with the intent of protecting retail merchants and their employees from civil suits filed against them in the course of conducting their lawful business practices. Retailers have a distinct privilege among businesses in being able to rely on such statutes as they pursue their property rights.

In a case in which a merchant detention statute was relied upon by the defendant as the central basis for the defense of his actions, the court found, among other things, that the business was not a retail business in the usual sense of the word and that the business could not rely on merchant protection statutes for protection in an action that a trial court found to be unlawful. Based on the finding that the defendant had acted unlawfully, the jury returned a verdict assessing damages for the false imprisonment that had occurred as a result of his actions.

In the case of *Huskinson v. Vanderheiden*, Huskinson was a truck driver who had been hired by a railroad materials firm to pick up and deliver steel rails pursuant to a contract executed between Vanderheiden's firm and the materials firm. The contract specified that the materials firm would pick up steel rails and transport them to a nearby mill, where they would be weighed and then shipped to the materials firm. A $20,000 down payment was made, with the understanding that multiple shipments would have to be completed until such time as the weight of the accumulated steel was equal to the value of the down payment. After $20,000 worth of steel had been picked up, the agreement called for no additional removal of steel from the premises until such time as the balance owed for steel valued in excess of the down payment had been paid.

Reportedly, the procedure involving the steel's removal, weighing, and shipping was followed for sixteen shipments. It was during Huskinson's seventeenth shipment that the cumulative value of the steel picked up exceeded the amount of the down payment. Indeed, the value of the seventeenth load apparently triggered an additional payment due to Vanderheiden's firm in the amount of $725.

Testimony by those involved in this case conflicted. Vanderheiden claimed that he asked Huskinson not to leave town until payment for the load had been made and that Huskinson agreed. Huskinson claimed that he had not discussed the matter with Vanderheiden.

Still, Huskinson checked into a local motel, where he stayed the night. He left with the load the next morning. Around noon, Huskinson was stopped by the state police, transported to the sheriff's office, and held for two hours. Testimony indicated that Vanderheiden had alerted the state police to the fact that a load of steel had been taken from town without payment. Reportedly, he supplied a description and the license number of the truck, and requested that the driver be apprehended.

Subsequent to his detention, Huskinson filed suit for false arrest and imprisonment against Vanderheiden and his employer. The trial judge entered a judgment after the jury's verdict in favor of Huskinson. Vanderheiden appealed the jury verdict and the judgment.

The Supreme Court of Nebraska noted that the evidence supported the fact that title to the steel had passed to Huskinson's employer, and as a result, the crime of grand larceny had not been committed. Regardless of whether payment was owed, title to the goods had passed. Huskinson had the right to leave town as he wished. Given that the title to the goods had passed to the buyer and that Huskinson's arrest was deemed unlawful, Vanderheiden was liable. The state's merchant detention statute was enacted to protect merchants from shoplifters, and as such was seen not to apply. The judgment of the district court was affirmed. The arrest was unlawful. Vanderheiden had initiated an unlawful imprisonment and as such was held civilly liable for his actions.

The great majority of states' merchant protection statutes state that privileged detentions must be for no more than a reasonable period of time. So long as probable cause exists to believe a crime has been committed or is being committed on retail premises and the detention is conducted in a reasonable manner and for a reasonable period of time, the merchant or his employees will be protected from paying civil damages to persons who claim they were injured as a result of an investigatory detention. The concern that arises and is the focus of this chapter is the term "reasonable" as it applies to the duration of a detention. In addition, the question as to when the clock stops on an apprehension begs to be answered. In other words, does a detention end when a merchant calls police? Does a detention end when the police arrive and take the person into custody? Does the detention end when the person is booked into jail? If one is to determine whether or not the duration of a detention is reasonable, then one must determine when the detention ends in order to assess its reasonableness. Such questions were raised and addressed in the case of *Cooke v. J. J. Newberry & Company*.

In *Cooke*, the question as to whether or not a detention was reasonable as regards the length of the detention became the central focus of the case. Cooke reportedly had shopped at several stores prior to entering Newberry's store. There, a security guard observed Cooke place a pair of stretch pants into another store's bag that Cooke possessed. The guard was informed by a sales clerk that Cooke had not paid for the pants. Once Cooke was outside the store, the guard approached her and inquired about the pants. Cooke admitted to not having paid for the pants and offered to pay for them at that time.

The guard refused to accept payment and asked that she accompany him to his office located in the store. She did so. Once there, the guard emptied the contents of her bag and discovered items with price tags attached from two other stores. He then checked to see if Cooke had an arrest record; she did not have one. At this point, the guard asked Cooke to sign a form admitting she had taken the pants without payment. Cooke refused to sign the form. The guard then called police. After police arrived, Cooke purportedly signed the form, indicating that she felt pressured to do so. Police took Cooke into custody. After being acquitted at trial on a charge of larceny, Cooke sued Newberry's.

The length of Cooke's detention in the store was a point of contention, and testimony about its duration conflicted. Cooke estimated that the length of the detention in the store was approximately one-half hour. The guard's estimate of thirty-five to forty minutes was similar. From the time Cooke was stopped outside the store until the time police arrived, the detention was arguably less than one hour. It was estimated that from the time she was stopped until police were called, twenty-seven minutes had elapsed. Cooke was detained at police headquarters for some time while she was being booked for larceny. At her trial for larceny, Cooke was acquitted and responded with a suit claiming damages arising from a false arrest and false imprisonment. Among Cooke's charges was the claim that the detention had been unreasonable in that it had been unreasonably long.

The case, tried in New Jersey, required much scrutiny utilizing the state's merchant detention statute. The New Jersey statute (NJ.S.A. 2A § 170-100) includes the statement that a merchant possessing "probable cause for believing that a person has willfully concealed unpurchased merchandise and that he can recover such merchandise by taking the person into custody, may for the purpose of attempting to effect such recovery, take the person into custody and detain him in a reasonable manner for not more than a reasonable time." That section of the statute concludes that taking a person into custody pursuant to the act will not render the merchant criminally or civilly liable. Cooke's civil suit against the store claimed her detention had been unreasonable, partly due to the fact that the duration of the detention had been for more than a reasonable period of time. The civil trial court disagreed and found for the merchant, and Cooke appealed.

The appellate division of the Superior Court of New Jersey held that the detention by the defendant, which lasted approximately twenty-seven minutes (the time elapsed between the apprehension of Cooke and the call to police), had not been an unreasonable length of time. The court refused to factor in the time between the call to the police and the arrival of officers or the time Cooke spent in police custody, finding that the detention had been lawful. The guard saw the plaintiff place the pants in the bag. The clerk stated that the plaintiff had not paid for the pants. Upon questioning, the plaintiff admitted to taking the merchandise without payment. She possessed a bag, which testimony purported was a common practice among shoplifters. Probable cause to detain and call police existed.

In addition, the court rejected the claim that the store did not enjoy the civil immunity offered under the merchant detention statute covering shoplifting because Cooke had not been charged with shoplifting but with larceny. The court found that the merchant detention statute did provide immunity in this instance, since the detention had been based on cause and conducted in a reasonable manner and for a reasonable period of time. The legal process, which provides that the prosecutor and not the retail merchant determine the appropriate charge to levy in criminal cases, was not lost on the court's reasoning. The court noted that it is up to the merchant to decide as the result of a reasonable investigation whether to call police and press charges or to let a suspect go. Such had been done.

Based on his observation, information from the clerk indicating that no payment had been made by Cooke, and Cooke's admission that she took the pants, the guard had reasonable grounds on which to prefer charges. Granted, he could have allowed the plaintiff to have paid for the pants after her detention, but it is the prerogative of a retailer, given a reasonable investigation, interrogation, and the facts available, to decide to prosecute or not to prosecute. Given that the length of time Cooke was detained was deemed reasonable by the court and that the detention was reasonable, the court found that the store employee had acted in good faith. The trial court found that the merchant detention statute did apply to the situation, even though the charge was larceny. Given all of the factors weighing in the decision, the finding of probable cause, and the finding of a reasonable investigation, it is not surprising that the trial court's finding for the store was upheld by the appellate court.

In regard to the *Cooke* case, it is important to realize that the fact that someone is found innocent at a criminal trial on shoplifting or larceny or that prior to a trial charges are dropped does not necessarily result in the store becoming vulnerable to paying civil damages allegedly incurred during a detention. A finding of innocence in a criminal trial does not equate with a direct relationship between the verdict and the presence of probable cause. A verdict may or may not indicate that a store's employees acted without probable cause and in an unreasonable manner. The verdict and the presence or absence of probable cause do not sufficiently establish a cause and effect relationship. Merchant detention statutes are explicit when they state that a store employee who possesses probable cause to believe a crime is being committed or was committed, who believes that an apprehension and investigation may result in the recovery of unpurchased store merchandise, and who conducts an investigation to effect such recovery in a reasonable manner and for not more than a reasonable period of time will not be held civilly liable for damages alleged to have incurred as a result of a detention.

Merchant protection statutes do not specify that retailers must prefer charges against everyone who is detained as a result of a shoplifting investigation. Merchant protection statutes do not specify that a privileged detention will be the result of obtaining a guilty verdict. Indeed, in *W. T. Grant Company v. Guercio*, the appellate court reversed the lower court finding and remanded the case for a new trial, finding that the trial court's instruction to the jury that it "could infer lack of probable cause" on the part of the store from an acquittal was a reversible error. The statutes offer their protection when probable cause is shown to have existed and when an investigation was conducted in a reasonable manner and for a reasonable period of time. As security guards will attest, most detentions do not result in guilty verdicts. Indeed, in the United States in a given year, it is estimated that only one in seven people actually apprehended for an investigation of shoplifting will actually be prosecuted, and of those, not all will be found guilty. Merchant protection statutes do not expect that everyone who is stopped will be prosecuted.

The law leaves it up to a merchant to ascertain whether or not he or she wishes to pursue a prosecution. As was mentioned in an earlier chapter, store managers need to assess each case on its own merits before deciding whether or not to press charges. In many cases, especially cases where a person's age or diminished mental abilities enter into the assessment, a store manager may accomplish more by not prosecuting those apprehended than by prosecuting. Merchants recognize the value of prosecuting shoplifters and in publicizing such a stance. They also recognize that while prosecution is a strong weapon in the fight against shoplifting, it is a weapon that must be utilized selectively, intelligently, and with reason.

Another suit pursued by an individual who was detained as a potential shoplifter had two twists that have not been seen in the other cases cited in this book. In the case of *Gonzales v. Harris*, it was seen that Gonzales was detained while the store itself was searched to see if he might have concealed merchandise in the store, as opposed to having concealed merchandise on himself. In addition, a request by Gonzales for a trial continuance, submitted two days before the trial ostensibly because he was incarcerated in a Mexican jail and could not appear for the trial, placed a second, new twist to the types of cases presented here. In addition, and of particular importance in this chapter, was the finding that the detention, which lasted approximately fifteen minutes and included a search of personal belongings as well as a search of the store, was found to be reasonable.

Testimony by both sides conflicted as to the course of events that led to the suit. In general, though, it was reported that Gonzales was shopping in a drugstore where Harris worked. Harris reported to the manager that he thought he saw Gonzales conceal an article of merchandise in his coat pocket. The manager then ordered another employee to watch Gonzales until the manager could exit the rear of the store, circle around to the front, and catch Gonzales as he left the store. Testimony indicated that the store employees failed to monitor continuously Gonzales's movements and actions while he remained in the store. Gonzales did make a purchase and exit the store, whereupon the manager stopped him and asked that he return to the store.

The series of events that followed were in dispute. Gonzales claimed that after they returned to the store, the manager asked that he empty his pockets. The manager, on the other hand, claimed that he asked Gonzales to go to the rear of the store, where they could talk. However, customers testifying in the case reported that immediately upon entering, Gonzales kicked off his shoes, turned his pants pockets inside out, and handed his coat over to the manager. No store merchandise was found on Gonzales. The manager allegedly yelled across the store to Harris and inquired as to where Gonzales had hidden the merchandise. Harris responded that he thought he saw Gonzales conceal something in his right coat pocket. After a search, the manager found nothing. He then told Gonzales to stay in the front of the store while he searched that portion of the store where the manager believed Gonzales might have hidden the merchandise. After a fruitless search, Gonzales asked that police be called and indicated he would sue the store. The manager ordered Gonzales to leave the store and never return.

Subsequently, Gonzales filed suit, seeking damages for false imprisonment and slander. The trial court found for the store and its employees. Specifically, Colorado's merchant detention statute entitled the manager to conduct a reasonable search based on probable cause. The activities related to the detention were seen as reasonable. Since the detention took less than fifteen minutes and was found to have been conducted in a reasonable manner, the court found that the store had not abused its privilege to apprehend and detain Gonzales. Refusing the request for a continuance, even given the fact that the plaintiff was incarcerated, was within the discretion of the court. The Colorado Court of Appeals affirmed the lower court finding for the store's employee.

It is interesting to note that the detention took less than fifteen minutes. How long is reasonable? The court found the detention as described to be reasonable and for a reasonable period of time. The meaning of "reasonable" often depends on the circumstances. Since the store employees had probable cause to believe that the plaintiff had hidden merchandise, they were within their rights to investigate. Again, it is not necessary that someone be found guilty of retail theft in order for the protection offered through merchant detention statutes to apply. Still, the concept of probable cause should be at the basis of every investigation, and the concept of reasonableness should drive every detention and investigation.

The question of probable cause and whether an apprehension was based on such is at the heart of most every suit related to a shoplifting investigatory detention. In *Godwin v. Gibson Products Company of Albany, Inc.*, the question of probable cause arose and was addressed. It was also seen that an investigation that lasted a short while was viewed as being of sufficiently reasonable duration as to be privileged.

In *Gibson*, testimony revealed that Godwin was in the Gibson store and in possession of a bottle of toiletries when he was confronted by the store's floorwalker (security guard). The floorwalker reported that Gibson was squatting down away from the cosmetics counter and appeared to be placing the bottle of cologne under his arm, where it would then be concealed under the coat worn by the plaintiff. The floorwalker, mentioning shoplifting, asked Godwin to accompany him to the office at the rear of the store. Once there, Godwin allegedly claimed he would not do it again. He produced his driver's license for identification. He was held without force and was never abused. The manager of the store typed up a statement that could be construed to be a form of confession and asked Godwin to read and sign it if the information it contained was correct. Godwin signed the statement.

After Godwin signed the statement, police officers were called. Two officers arrived and took Godwin into custody. The store manager indicated to the officers that he wished to have Godwin prosecuted. The length of the detention, including the time it took police to arrive, was estimated to have lasted less than forty minutes. Godwin was taken to police headquarters, where a formal warrant was obtained and Godwin was booked. Later, Godwin filed suit claiming that the store had lacked probable cause to detain him, and he sought damages for false imprisonment and malicious prosecution.

The superior court, in reviewing the facts of the case, granted the store's request for summary judgment. Godwin appealed the granting of summary judgment, again stressing that the store had lacked probable cause to detain him. The Court of Appeals of Georgia affirmed the superior court's granting of summary judgment, noting that the employees of the store did possess probable cause to believe the crime of shoplifting was being committed. Specifically, the court noted that it would appear to a prudent man that Godwin's squatting down and placing the cologne under his coat was conduct that would cause a reasonable person to believe that Godwin was in the process of committing the offense of shoplifting. Since probable cause existed and the investigation that ensued, including Godwin's signing the statement admitting to the concealment of the merchandise, was conducted in a reasonable manner, Godwin was not entitled to recover for damages alleged to have been incurred during the detention.

As Godwin discovered, Georgia's merchant detention statute states that when a merchant, his agent, or his employee causes "to be detained or arrested, any person reasonably thought to be engaged in shoplifting and, as a result of such detention or arrest, the person so detained or arrested shall institute suit for false arrest or false imprisonment against such owner, operator, agent or employee, no recovery shall be had by the plaintiff in such action where it is established by competent evidence that the plaintiff had so conducted himself, or behaved in such manner, as to cause a man of reasonable prudence to believe that such plaintiff was committing the offense of shoplifting." Godwin's actions, including his squatting away from the counter and placing the cologne under his coat, were seen as conduct that would lead a reasonably prudent person to believe that the act of shoplifting was being committed. Godwin received nothing for his efforts.

A case involving the sounding of an electronic alarm also involved questions of reasonableness as to the length of the detention. In *Dent v. May Department Stores Company*, Dent sued May for damages related to Dent's alleged false imprisonment and false arrest.

It was reported that as Dent was leaving the department store, an electronic alarm sounded. A security guard working for the store approached Dent and asked if she had made any purchases in the store. Dent, who was carrying several bags, responded affirmatively. Dent allowed the guard to look at the skirt she had just purchased, which was in the department store's bag along with the receipt indicating its purchase. The guard noted that the clerk had failed to remove the electronic alarm tag and asked if Dent would follow him to an office. Purportedly, the guard indicated that such incidents occurred frequently and that there was no problem. Once in the room, the guard used the tag removal machine, wrote a short report about the incident, and returned the skirt to Dent, and she was allowed to leave.

Dent filed suit claiming false arrest and false imprisonment. Dent claimed that several people witnessed her detention near the exit and that she overheard some of them saying a shoplifter had been caught. Testimony indicated that the entire detention lasted well under one hour. The guard did not injure Dent, though it was claimed that after asking Dent to return to the store, he began to touch Dent's elbow with his hand, whereupon Dent indicated that such was not necessary as she accompanied the guard to the office. At trial, the store moved for summary judgment, claiming its employee had acted on probable cause and that his actions had been reasonable and concluded in a reasonable period of time. Summary judgment was entered on behalf of the store, as the trial court ruled that as a matter of law, no false arrest or imprisonment had occurred. Dent appealed the judgment.

On appeal, the appellate court noted that the existence of probable cause is a mixed question of both law and fact. When the facts related to the existence of probable cause are not in dispute, the question as to the existence of probable cause is one of law. The court noted that even if the actions of the guard were construed as confining Dent, the actions were based on probable cause (the sounding of the alarm). The sounding of the alarm was sufficient to support the guard's belief that merchandise was being removed from the store without payment.

However, despite the guard having probable cause, the court noted that a detention, even one based on probable cause, could still constitute false imprisonment if the detention were conducted in an unreasonable manner or for an unreasonable length of time. The appellate court noted that the guard's actions were reasonable in that he asked Dent if she would accompany him to the office to have the tag removed, quickly filled out the incident report in her presence, explained the problem, returned the skirt to her, and allowed her to leave. Also of importance here was the fact that the court found that the short length of time Dent had been detained was reasonable. Given that the detention was based on probable cause, was conducted in a reasonable manner, and was for no longer than a reasonable period of time, the appellate court affirmed the trial court's summary judgment in favor of the store.

In a Louisiana case, the court found that damages that had allegedly been incurred as a result of a purported detention could not be recovered since, according to the court, a detention had not occurred. The case, *Eason v. J. Weingarten, Inc.*, resulted in the actions of the grocery store's employees being found reasonable and their inquiry conducted in a reasonable manner. Indeed, the actions of the employees were not deemed a detention by the court, and as such, no damage award could ensue.

In *Eason*, it was reported that a manager of the Weingarten's grocery store located in Lake Charles, Louisiana, observed Eason and her daughter shopping. Each was pushing her own grocery cart. The daughter's cart contained Eason's grandchild in the built-in seat. The manager observed that as they went through the produce section of the store, Eason handed some grapes to the infant, who began eating them. Continuing to observe the two, Eason noted that they opened two bags of potato chips and began eating them as they continued to shop. Believing that they might not pay for the items, the manager decided to continue to observe them.

A short time later, the manager testified, he saw Eason remove a bottle of hair dye from the drug counter shelf and place it into her open purse, which she then closed and placed in her cart's child seat. At about this time, the manager asked another store employee to join him in observing Eason, indicating that he was suspicious of her actions. The two store employees observed Eason as best as they could, given the fact that they were trying not to alert her to the fact that they suspected she might be taking merchandise without intending to pay for it. On one aisle, Eason reportedly removed the dye from her cart and placed it back onto a store shelf. The store employees did not observe Eason placing the dye on the shelf, as they were not in a position to see her at that point.

The two store employees continued to observe Eason as she checked out. At the checkout counter, the manager stood by and watched to see if Eason would pay for hair dye. She did not. She also did not pay for the grapes the child had eaten. Eason was placing groceries in her car when the two store employees approached her, indicated they needed to talk with her, and asked that she return to the store. Eason agreed and returned to the store with the two employees. Once there, she was directed into an office at the front of the store where no one could overhear them.

The store manager asked Eason to open her purse, and she did. The manager asked Eason what she had done with the bottle of hair dye she had removed from the drug counter. Eason acknowledged taking a bottle of dye from the counter, but insisted that she placed it next to her purse, which was in the baby seat of her cart. She claimed that she had not placed the dye in her purse, and she denied that at that point she had even opened her purse. Eason told the manager that she had decided not to buy the dye, had removed it from her cart, and had placed it on another shelf in the store. She took the two to the shelf, where the dye was clearly visible. Once there, according to the manager, Eason asked if she was being accused of stealing and threatened to call the police. The manager offered to call the police for her, noting that she had not paid for the grapes. Eason admitted to not having paid for the grapes but said she had not realized that giving the child grapes while shopping would cause a problem. She offered to pay for the grapes. The manager stated that everything was okay, that they were even. At this point, Eason supposedly wanted to return her groceries for a refund, a request that was turned down by the store manager. Eason reportedly then called a lawyer, left the store with her groceries, and subsequently filed suit.

Taking a different tack than that taken in most of the cases cited in this book, Eason did not claim that she was unlawfully detained. She claimed that she suffered damages as a result of defamatory remarks made to her by the store manager. She claimed that others in the store could "see what was going on" and that as a result she was embarrassed and humiliated. Further, she claimed that her daughter could hear the accusations of the store manager.

The store manager claimed that his remarks were reasonable. His testimony indicated that he had not detained Eason against her will, that she had agreed to return to the store, that he took care in conducting a discreet inquiry, that no customers could have overheard his inquiry, and that Eason had not been embarrassed nor humiliated. Finally, the store manager claimed that the actions he and his employee took pursuant to an investigation of what they believed to be a theft were reasonable and privileged under Louisiana's law.

The trial judge agreed with the store employees. The judge concluded that Eason had not been detained against her will and that she had freely returned to the store. No force had been used to return Eason to the store; nor had force been used to detain her. Each of Eason's actions was voluntary, even that of allowing her purse to be searched while in the office. In short, the trial court found that the store employees had conducted a reasonable, simple, lawful inquiry into what they believed to be a retail theft, and found in favor of the store.

The Court of Appeals of Louisiana, Third District, agreed that Eason had not been held against her will. However, the appellate court addressed another question, which was whether or not the comments by the manager were damaging. In addition, the court had to decide whether such comments were privileged. The court noted that even though the manager never accused Eason of stealing, his actions indicated that he believed she had. In other words, actions sometimes speak louder than words. The court noted that the unspoken accusation was false and defamatory; Eason had not stolen the hair dye. The last and most important question, though, is whether the manager's unspoken accusation, coupled with the inquiry, was privileged under the state's merchant detention statute.

The court found that reasonable grounds existed for the store employees to conduct an investigation. There was probable cause to detain Eason for a reasonable period of time for the purpose of conducting a reasonable investigation of the matter. The court found that even though probable cause existed to allow the investigation and store employees conducted a reasonable investigation, no detention had in fact occurred. Eason voluntarily went back to the store, voluntarily opened her purse, and volunteered the information as to where she returned the dye to the shelf. The store manager was shown to have conducted a reasonable investigation and to have taken care to prevent others from overhearing his discussion with Eason in order to prevent any embarrassment to her. The appellate court agreed with the lower court that Eason could not recover damages based on the reasonable inquiry as conducted. The court further noted that it was not necessary to consider whether or not the "detention" was privileged under Louisiana's merchant detention statute, since it concluded that no detention had occurred and that the store had not incurred liability from its employees' actions regardless of the state's protection statute.

The length of a detention matters. It was interesting to note that the court ruled in Eason that "no detention" had occurred. It obviously follows that if no detention occurred, then the length of the detention becomes a moot point. Still, it must be remembered that state statutes expect detentions to be reasonable and for no more than a reasonable period of time.

Store managers and retail employees have heard every excuse imaginable as to why someone took merchandise without payment. Statements to the effect that "a store charges too much" or "since I shop here all of the time, the store owes me something" or "it was just a bonus for my spending my money here" and the like have often been used in attempts to rationalize the taking of retail merchandise without payment. Such rationalizations may have varying levels of substance and as such may deserve some consideration. However, most do not possess substance. In the case of *DeMarie v. Jefferson Stores, Inc.*, the plaintiff claimed that the reason he didn't pay for the goods, essentially, was that he was entitled to exchange the goods for defective ones he had purportedly purchased earlier. A store clerk had not allowed an exchange, as DeMarie did not have a receipt in his possession, a requisite that Jefferson Stores expected in order to facilitate an exchange of goods. It was the inability of DeMarie to obtain a refund or exchange and his subsequent actions that led to legal problems for DeMarie.

Testimony in *DeMarie* indicated that DeMarie had purchased wall fasteners at Jefferson's. The type of fasteners DeMarie purchased allow a screw to be used in sheet rock or paneling via the insertion of a plastic sleeve into predrilled holes. DeMarie claimed that as he inserted the sleeves, they collapsed, making them useless for the purpose at hand. It was reported that he returned to Jefferson's, approached a cashier, and mentioned to her that he had purchased a package of fasteners that apparently were defective and that he wished to exchange the fasteners. He was told he would need to have his receipt in order to execute an exchange. He did not have his receipt, and so he entered the store to shop.

DeMarie is said to have selected several items as he walked through the store. Reportedly, he took a package of fasteners from a display shelf, removed the fasteners from their cellophane package, and placed them in his pocket. The package of fasteners was priced at less than one dollar. As DeMarie was allegedly doing this, a security employee of Jefferson's was observing his actions. He reported seeing DeMarie drop the empty package to the floor and place the fasteners in his pocket. DeMarie then went to the checkout area, paid for his other selections, and exited the store. Immediately, he was approached by Jefferson security employees and asked to return to the store. He was taken to an office and questioned about the fasteners.

DeMarie apparently recounted his experience with the defective fasteners and his conversation with the cashier, and purportedly admitted to not paying for the fasteners. The guards did not confirm DeMarie's story with the cashier but instead called police, who quickly arrived and took DeMarie into custody. DeMarie was booked for petty theft. Dade County (Florida), where the trial took place, has a Pretrial Intervention and Advocate Program, which DeMarie successfully completed, and as a consequence, his prosecution for petty theft was terminated. Subsequently, DeMarie filed suit against Jefferson Stores, alleging false arrest and malicious prosecution. Specifically, DeMarie raised the argument that the guards' unwillingness to confirm his story with the cashier was unreasonable. He charged that the guards should have confirmed his side of the story with the cashier prior to calling police.

DeMarie's civil trial against Jefferson Stores resulted in a judgment for Jefferson. Perhaps not surprisingly, the jury found that probable cause did exist for the guards to initiate a detention of DeMarie and that the store employees' actions were justified. The detention was conducted in a reasonable manner and for a reasonable length of time. In short, the actions of the store employees were reasonable, lawful, and privileged.

On appeal, the District Court of Appeals of Florida, Third District, affirmed the lower court's findings and held for the store. The appellate court noted that DeMarie himself had admitted his intent to take the fasteners without payment. In this instance, even if the guards had checked with the cashier to confirm DeMarie's chronology of events, the most the cashier could have said was that indeed she had told DeMarie he was not entitled to a refund or exchange for the fasteners without a receipt. So even if the guards had been armed with that information, DeMarie's actions would still have given rise to a probable cause to detain him by store security. Again, DeMarie's ready admission of his intent not to pay for the fasteners and the fact that he felt entitled to the fasteners were not lost on the court.

The appellate court noted that probable cause existed to detain De-Marie. Since probable cause was found to have existed and the detention was shown to have been reasonable and for a reasonable period of time, the store's employees were found to have acted lawfully in the protection of their store's property. Since the detention was justified, the charges of false arrest and malicious prosecution failed. The store prevailed in its efforts. It is important to recognize that the Jefferson Stores employees were acting on probable cause. It is important to recognize that they acted in a reasonable manner. It is important to recognize that their investigation was concluded in a reasonable period of time.

To reiterate, store employees have heard every conceivable rationale for the taking of retail merchandise without payment. Some of these rationales are with foundation. As is seen elsewhere in this book, some people innocently forget to pay for merchandise or innocently conceal the merchandise without an intent to defraud a merchant. However, as is true in other cases, the willful concealment of merchandise to avoid payment is sometimes an attempt to act on a rationalization that the store "owes" the customer, in some manner. Whether the theft is committed because of the customer's prior patronage, because the store charges too much, or because the customer is trying to get even in some other manner, the resulting impact on an employee's actions should be the same. Employees should act on probable cause, should behave reasonably, and if a detention is necessary, should complete it in a reasonable period of time. Reasonableness should drive employee actions. Probable cause should initiate such actions. Without these two factors, retail investigations leave a store vulnerable. With them, stores and their employees will enjoy the protection offered by merchant protection statutes.

Many stores try to get individuals apprehended and detained for questioning to sign a waiver of liability form indicating that they will not sue the store for pursuing its property interest. Sometimes individuals apprehended and detained will sign such a form. Often, though, those detained balk at such a suggestion. Still, when a person signs such a form, does it protect the store from being held civilly liable for an unlawful detention?

The question as to whether individuals may sign away their right to sue was one of the questions raised in the case of *Chelette v. Wal-Mart Stores, Inc.* In *Chelette*, it was seen that having an apprehended individual sign a statement holding a store harmless does not necessarily protect the store from civil suits when the apprehension involved was illegal. In this case, Chelette was observed by a security guard paying for her purchases in a shopping cart. Along with numerous items in the cart were Chelette's two small children and a bag of charcoal on the lower shelf. The guard believed that Chelette did not bring the bag of charcoal to the attention of the cashier.

As Chelette began to exit the store, the guard informed her that she had not paid for the charcoal in the cart and asked that she accompany him to the back of the store to discuss the matter. After consulting with the store manager, the guard then had Chelette sign a release of any causes of action she might have taken against Wal-Mart, in return for which Wal-Mart agreed not to sue plaintiff for civil conversion. Chelette was allowed to pay for the charcoal and then escorted from the store. Reportedly, she was detained fifteen minutes.

Chelette later filed a false imprisonment suit against Wal-Mart and its security guard for damages caused by her detention for suspicion of shoplifting. The lower court refused Wal-Mart's request for a summary judgment and entered a judgment for Chelette after a trial on the merits. The Court of Appeals of Louisiana, Third District, affirmed the decision, noting among other factors that the store did not have reasonable cause to detain Chelette for shoplifting under the facts presented. Among the more noteworthy factors was the fact that the cashier had overlooked the charcoal, too. Chelette paid $47 for her other purchases. The court noted that Chelette had made no attempt to conceal the charcoal. And lastly, there appeared to be no intent to shoplift. The court found that the customer's consent to the release of her legal claims against the store was vitiated by duress. The duress arose from the fact that Chelette felt she could not leave unless she signed the form and the guard's statement that he was prepared to use reasonable force to detain Chelette, if necessary.

It is apparent that if the apprehension and arrest are not lawful, then the merchant or the merchant's agents will lose the protection they enjoy from merchant protection statutes. A merchant and others involved in retail security need to know and follow the applicable state statutes as they apply to apprehending and detaining shoplifting suspects. An unlawful detention, regardless of how short, will be found to be unlawful and place a store and its employees at risk. Having a customer sign a waiver of liability concerning an illegal detention will not remove the liability that follows an unlawful detention.

Table 5.1
Citations and Management Implications in Chapter Five

Case	Implication
Schmidt v. Richman Gordman, Inc. and Horan; Clifton v. Richman Gordman, Inc. and Horan, 215 N.W.2d 105 (Neb. 1974)	Detentions that are deemed unreasonable in duration may leave a store vulnerable. Statutes specify that detentions be for a reasonable time. Prosecutions without sufficient cause may be deemed unreasonable.
Wal-Mart Stores, Inc. v. Yarbrough, 681 S.W.2d 359 (Ark. 1984)	Stores should have lawful procedures that employees are expected to follow when conducting detentions. Employees should know and adhere to such procedures.
Weissman v. K-Mart Corporation, 396 So.2d 1164 (Fla. 3DCA 1981)	Detentions without probable cause will not be seen as reasonable. If probable cause ceases to exist, then the privilege to detain ceases to exist.
City of Pensacola v. Owens, 369 So.2d 238 (Fla. 1979)	Where prudence dictates further investigation, liability may arise from one's failure to conduct further investigation.
West v. Wal-Mart Stores, Inc., 539 So.2d 1258 (La.App. 3Cir. 1989)	Detentions of short duration that are not based on sufficient cause will be deemed unreasonable. Detentions, even of short duration, must be based on probable cause. An unprivileged detention leaves a store vulnerable.
Gibson's Products, Inc. v. Edwards, 247 S.E.2d 183 (Ga.App. 1978)	When the facts are in dispute, the existence of probable cause will be a question for the jury to decide. Compensatory and punitive damages may be awarded in cases of false imprisonment and malicious prosecution.
People v. Lee, 204 Cal.Rptr. 667 (Cal.Super. 1984)	Detentions must be reasonable. Reasonableness is a central tenet to a privileged detention.
Southwest Drug Stores of Mississippi, Inc. v. Garner, 195 So.2d 837 (Miss. 1967)	Before initiating a detention, probable cause needs to be established. An investigation into facts that would bear on whether probable cause may exist should be conducted prior to detaining an individual.

(Continued)

Table 5.1 (*Continued*)

Case	Implication
Huskinson v. Vanderheiden, 251 N.W.2d 144 (Neb. 1977)	An individual who initiates an unlawful arrest may be held civilly liable for the detention. Merchant detention statutes were enacted to protect merchants who lawfully pursue their property rights against individuals they believe are shoplifting.
Cooke v. J. J. Newberry and Company, 232 A.2d 425 (N.J. 1967)	An investigation must be reasonable and for a reasonable period of time. A person does not have to be found guilty of shoplifting for a store and its employees to enjoy the protection offered by merchant protection statutes.
W. T. Grant Company v. Guercio, 238 A.2d 855 (Md.App. 1968)	One cannot infer a lack of probable cause because an apprehension fails to result in criminal conviction in a shoplifting-related case.
Gonzales v. Harris, 528 P.2d 259 (Colo.App. 1974)	A reasonable detention that is for a reasonable period of time and based on probable cause will not subject a store to civil liability. Once a plaintiff agrees to accept a court-ordered judgment and not pursue further litigation, the plaintiff cannot seek further court intervention.
Godwin v. Gibson Products Company of Albany, Inc., 172 S.E.2d 467 (Ga.App. 1970)	A short-duration investigation based on probable cause will be deemed to be reasonable and the investigation considered privileged under merchant detention statutes.
Dent v. May Department Stores Company, 459 A.2d 1042 (D.C.App. 1982)	A detention may constitute false imprisonment even when initiated on probable cause if the detention is conducted in an unreasonable manner or for an unreasonable length of time.
Eason v. J. Weingarten, Inc., 219 So.2d 516 (La.App. 3Cir. 1969)	A reasonable investigation is privileged. Damages do not normally ensue when a detention has not been conducted. Reasonableness is paramount in the conduct of an investigation.

Table 5.1 (*Continued*)

Case	Implication
DeMarie v. Jefferson Stores, Inc., 442 So.2d 1014 (Fla.App. 3Dist. 1983)	An individual cannot unilaterally remove merchandise from a store with the intent of not paying and expect not to have to answer for such actions.
Chelette v. Wal-Mart Stores, Inc., 535 So.2d 558 (La.App. 3Cir. 1988)	An unlawful detention, regardless of how short in time, is still unlawful. Having a customer sign a civil liability waiver does not always protect a store, especially if it concerns an unlawful detention and can be construed to have been signed under duress.

SUMMARY OF CONCEPTS IN CHAPTER FIVE

1. Most merchant detention statutes specify that detentions not be for a longer period of time than is reasonable in order for the detention to be privileged and civil liability immunity to ensue. Louisiana's statute specifies that detentions by merchants must not exceed sixty minutes in order to be privileged.

2. If a detention is seen as unreasonably long, civil liability immunity will not ensue.

3. Any conduct not predicated on probable or sufficient cause that prevents an individual from going where he or she may lawfully go may be construed as an unlawful imprisonment.

4. An unlawful false imprisonment, regardless of duration, will result in a store losing its civil liability immunity.

5. When a legal proceeding is initiated against an individual by a merchant and the proceeding is not based on probable cause, and when there is a showing of malice on the part of the merchant resulting in damage or harm to the individual, the merchant may be found liable for a malicious prosecution.

6. A finding of malicious prosecution may result in the awarding of punitive damages.

7. A decision to prosecute or press charges should be made on a case-by-case basis. Not everyone who takes merchandise without payment intends to steal merchandise.

8. A detention conducted in an unreasonable manner will be found to be unlawful and unprivileged regardless of the duration.

9. Loud accusations made in public and without regard to the rights of an individual may be found to be unreasonable; they leave a store vulnerable.

10. Before apprehending and detaining an individual, one must have sufficient cause to believe that the individual is committing a crime or has committed a crime.

11. A privileged detention that imparts civil liability immunity does not require a finding of guilty in a criminal trial. Civil liability immunity requires only probable cause and reasonableness.

12. One cannot infer a lack of probable cause when an apprehension fails to result in a conviction.

13. Stores do not have to prosecute to enjoy civil liability immunity.

14. Reasonable investigations based on sufficient cause are privileged.

Chapter Six

Civil Recovery Laws

Shoplifters, by their very acts of theft, cause harm to store owners. The tens of billions of dollars of lost merchandise is a direct cost that retail merchants in this country bear every year. The cost of prosecution, including the costs associated with the time in court that employees spend testifying in shoplifting cases is not inconsequential to many stores. Damage to merchandise caused by efforts to conceal the merchandise by shoplifters reduces the value of the merchandise to customers. In those cases, especially in the past, where the merchandise had to be kept by police as evidence, the storage of the merchandise in police evidence rooms for long periods of time often resulted in the merchandise being out of season or obsolete when finally returned to the retailer, again, reducing its value. The costs of prevention are also high, as stores turn to expensive technology, the hiring of security guards, and other costly steps to prevent or thwart thievery.

Yes, shoplifting costs stores money. Lots of money. Shoplifters harm merchants. Indeed, according to one estimate, one-third of retail bankruptcies are caused by excessive shoplifting. Shoplifting is costly. Since shoplifters harm retailers, can shoplifters be held financially responsible for their actions? Can they be counted on to bear part of the financial strain they cause retail stores? Well, yes, sometimes they can.

Store owners have always had the right to sue shoplifters. As individuals who have undoubtedly committed a harm against a merchant, shoplifters have been actionable for their thefts for years. However, the great majority of store owners have never even considered suing shoplifters, feeling that such action would cost too much and take too much time, that the nature of the harm the owner incurred would be difficult to prove, or in general, that such a course of action would not be worth the trouble. In some cases, especially in those cases in which the shoplifter suffered a financial hardship (some shoplifters are destitute), defendents would be unable to pay for the damages they caused. Facing these realities, many retailers in the past have refused to pursue their rights beyond getting back their merchandise and seeing that justice was done by prosecuting those apprehended for willful acts of shoplifting.

A few years back, having a shoplifter serve time in jail was the most that a store owner could hope to see as the result of his or her efforts to apprehend and detain shoplifters. In dealing with the shoplifting problem, most retailers have come to expect that shoplifters will seldom, if ever, see the inside of a jail. Of those that do spend time in jail, few will spend more than a few hours, and even then, usually those hours are spent in raising a bond that is normally modest. However, things have changed in recent years.

Since 1973, when the first state passed a merchant civil recovery law, state legislatures have gone beyond the implementation of simple merchant detention protection statutes and have allowed merchants to take the offensive. At the urging of business owners and organized business groups, legislatures across the country have adopted laws referred to as civil recovery laws. At this time, each of the fifty states has adopted such laws and it appears that, increasingly, they are serving as effective shoplifting deterrents and are reducing the cost of shoplifting deterrence. Specifically, civil recovery laws have been adopted with the purpose of assisting store owners in their fight to deter shoplifting by helping them recover some of the costs they incur as a result of the shoplifting problem. In addition, it was expected, and is being borne out, that civil recovery laws will be seen as a major deterrent to individuals who may consider shoplifting from retail merchants.

State civil recovery laws are simple, easily relied-upon statutes that allow retail merchants to demand recompense for their shoplifting-related costs from those individuals who have been apprehended taking merchandise from their premises. In its simplest form, civil recovery statutes allow store owners to write a simple civil demand letter to individuals apprehended for shoplifting and demand payment of a fee, that, ostensibly, is to help the merchant recover the costs associated with the crime.

Like merchant protection statutes, civil recovery statutes are state laws. As such, they vary in their wording, in the amount of money they allow to be demanded, in who is responsible for payment of the demand notice if a minor is involved, and in their general applicability. Since the specifics of civil recovery laws vary among the states and since over time they are subject to change within a given state, it is imperative that merchants seek the counsel of their attorneys when implementing a civil recovery process.

For expository purposes, Alabama's civil recovery statute is included in this chapter. It is important to note that most civil recovery statutes that deal with shoplifting are relatively recent, and as such have not had the numerous opportunities to be tested in court that merchant protection statutes have. As an example, Alabama's civil recovery statute was adopted only as recently as 1993 and as such has not been subject to judicial review. Still, early court challenges to civil recovery statutes that have surfaced have generally failed.

In *Payless Drug Stores v. Brown*, the Supreme Court of Oregon affirmed an appellate court ruling that found parents could be held civilly liable for theft acts committed by minor children. Specifically, arguments that the civil recovery act was vague, that parents should not be held liable for the actions of their children, that the amount allowed to be recovered under Oregon law was unrelated to the amount of actual damages incurred by the store, and that the civil recovery statute violated the due process rights of individuals were all shot down. The constitutionality of Oregon's civil recovery law was affirmed.

It is expected that should any problems surface with any particular state's statute, the legislature of that state will move to change the law so that its impact will not be negated. The swell of support in state legislatures for a simple, cost-effective tool on which retailers can rely for recompense will undoubtedly assure adoption of laws that will survive a court challenge.

The wording of Alabama's statute is shown below. Each part of Alabama's statute is shown in italics, with explanatory material following each part of the statute. Again, each state's statute is unique, though all have the same intent and, in many cases, almost the same wording. Merchants should obtain a copy of their state's civil recovery statute, read it, discuss it with their attorneys, and plan their recovery strategy accordingly. Like merchant protection statutes, civil recovery laws have stipulations that must be followed in order to gain the benefits that such laws offer. Failure to follow the law as specified may preclude the store from pursuing its property rights or, worse, may subject the store to action by the shoplifter.

AL ST §6-5-271 Liability for theft or attempted theft, liability of parents of unemancipated minor; liability for defrauding an eating establishment; liability of foster home.

(a) An adult or emancipated minor who commits or attempts to commit a theft of property consisting of goods for sale on the premises of a merchant in violation of Sections §13A-8-3, 13A-8-4, or 13A-8-5, shall be civilly liable to the merchant in an amount consisting of all of the following:

(1) The full retail value of the merchandise if not recovered in merchantable condition at its full retail price.

(2) Expenses for recovery of the merchandise in the amount of $200.

(3) Reasonable attorney's fees and court costs not to exceed $1,000.

In paragraph A of Alabama's statute, the statute clearly states that an adult who commits retail theft or an emancipated minor who commits retail theft shall be held civilly liable to the merchant. This section of the state law is explicit in its expectation that adults and emancipated minors should be held accountable for their actions. The sentence in this paragraph that notes that individuals guilty of "Sections §13A-8-3, 13A-8-4, or 13A-8-5" shall be civilly liable needs further explanation.

These three sections of Alabama law, Sections §13A-8-3, 13A-8-4, and 13A-8-5, concern the crime of property theft. A person guilty of §13A-8-3 is one that has been found guilty of taking property with a dollar value greater than $1,000. Section §13A-8-3 defines theft of property with a value exceeding $1,000 or the theft of a motor vehicle, regardless of its value, as theft in the first degree. Further, by statute, theft in the first degree is designated a Class B felony in the state of Alabama.

Section §13A-8-4 concerns theft of property in the second degree. Under Alabama law, the theft of property that exceeds $250 in value but does not exceed $1,000 in value is designated theft of property in the second degree. This section also stipulates that the theft of credit cards and the theft of guns, livestock, or controlled substances, regardless of their value, constitute theft of property in the second degree. Finally, a theft of property from retail premises exceeding $100 in value but having a value of less than $1,000, where the thief has previously been convicted of a theft in the first or second degree, constitutes a theft in the second degree. Theft of property in the second degree is designated a Class C felony.

Finally, §13A-8-5 stipulates that a theft of property from a retail merchant with a value of less than $250 constitutes a theft in the third degree. As was noted in §13A-8-4, a theft of an item valued in excess of $100 may be deemed a theft in the second degree if the thief was previously convicted of a theft in the first or second degree. Theft in the third degree is designated a Class A misdemeanor.

Alabama's civil recovery statute is similar to other state's statutes in that it delineates who is liable for payment, places limits on how much can be demanded by merchants, and specifies exceptions to the concept of blanket parental responsibility when a minor child (or other individual) has committed the act of shoplifting. In short, civil recovery statutes vary among the states, but they all state who is to be held responsible, they all place limitations on the amount of money that can be demanded, and they generally cover the concept of parental responsibility in those situations where minors are involved.

Paragraph A of the statute allows merchants to civilly demand the following from adult shoplifters: damages in the amount of the retail value of the merchandise, if it was not recovered in merchantable condition; expenses for recovery of the merchandise in the amount of $200; plus a reasonable amount to cover the store's legal fees, not to exceed $1,000. Thus, for an item valued at $25, a store could demand a maximum of $1,225 from the individual who was apprehended, assuming it had to seek legal counsel and the cost of such legal services was at least $1,000.

(b) Parents or legal guardians of an unemancipated minor under the age of 19 shall be liable in a civil action for the minor who commits or attempts to commit a theft of property consisting of goods for sale on the premises of a merchant in violation of Sections §13A-8-3, 13A-8-4, or 13A-8-5, to the merchant in an amount consisting of the following:

(1) The full retail value of the merchandise if not recovered in merchantable condition at its full retail price.

(2) Expenses for recovery of the merchandise in the amount of $200.

(3) Reasonable attorney's fees and court costs not to exceed $1,000.

(4) Parents or legal guardians of an unemancipated minor under the age of 19 shall only be liable in a civil action in any calendar year for up to three offenses under the provisions of this article with a maximum liability of $750 for each offense.

Paragraph B stipulates that parents or legal guardians of unemancipated minors under the age of 19 shall be liable in a civil action for the actions of the minor when the minor has committed or has attempted to commit a theft of goods held for sale by a retail merchant. While holding parents liable for the actions of their children, the state legislature did limit the liability of the parents for the actions of their children. Specifically, parents or legal guardians are liable to the merchant for the retail value of the merchandise at its normal price if it was not recovered in merchantable condition plus $200 for expenses the store incurs in recovering the merchandise. In addition, the store may recover attorney's fees and court costs, if necessary, in an amount not to exceed $1,000.

It should be noted that while parents are generally held to be responsible for the actions of their children, Alabama places a limit on such liability. The state's statute stipulates that the maximum parental liability for each offense is $750, and further, that parents have their responsibility for damages limited to paying a maximum of three such awards per year. The legislature obviously thought that there should be a limit as to what one might reasonably expect a parent to be held responsible for, given the misbehavior of children.

(c) A customer who orders a meal in a restaurant or other eating establishment, receives at least a portion thereof, and then leaves with the intent to defraud the eating establishment, without paying for the meal is subject to liability under this section, if such meal is received by the customer in a good and merchantable condition.

Alabama's law is not unique in recognizing that retail theft goes beyond the idea that an individual walks into a store and walks out with store merchandise for which payment was not made. Paragraph C stipulates that eating food in a restaurant and leaving without payment is actionable under the statute. A person who eats and then leaves without paying may be held civilly liable under this statute so long as the food received was of good and merchantable condition.

Restaurants are placed in the same victimization predicament as are stores when food is served and eaten with an intent on the part of the diner not to pay for the product consumed. Indeed, it is a rare restaurant that has not had individuals skip out without paying their bills. Taking food from restaurants without payment is a form of shoplifting. Merchandise has been taken without appropriate payment. It can be argued that restaurants are in a doubly precarious situation, since not only is the food taken without payment, but the cost of preparation, which can be substantial, has in a sense been stolen as well.

Civil recovery laws stipulate that parents of minors who commit theft of restaurant food will be held responsible for the deeds of their children. Again, as stipulated in Alabama's act, the parents of a minor who has taken food from a restaurant with the intent of defrauding the restaurant of rightful payment are civilly liable to the restaurant to the limits allowed. Again, in Alabama, such civil responsibility is limited to $750 per incident, and parents are responsible financially for a maximum of three such incidents per year.

(d) Persons operating a certified foster home are not liable under this section for the acts of children not related to them by blood or marriage who are under their care, nor shall parents or legal guardians whose child is not living with them or where the juvenile violates Sections §13A-8-3, 13A-8-4, or 13A-8-5, with the intent to make the parent or legal guardian liable, be held liable under this article.

Finally, it is interesting to note that Alabama's legislature decided to include a provision in the civil recovery statute that exempts certified foster parents from being held civilly liable for thefts by foster children under the care of the parents. Ostensibly, the legislature felt that to hold foster parents responsible for thefts committed by foster children would burden further what is often a difficult situation and, as such, elected to exempt foster parents from civil liability. Similarly, the legislature felt that noncustodial parents should not be held responsible for the actions of their children while living under the care of the other parent.

Certified foster parents can and will be held responsible for thefts of store merchandise or food from restaurants when the theft is committed by the blood-related children or by the marriage-related children of the foster parent. When a certified foster parent is held civilly liable for the theft acts of a minor who is related by blood or marriage, the provisions limiting the civil demand to $750 per incident applies.

In Alabama, as in most other states, the amount of money that can be civilly demanded varies according to the classification of the shoplifter. In Alabama, an adult can be held civilly liable for a maximum of $1,200 plus the value of the merchandise, should the merchandise not have been recovered in good, merchantable condition. Parents of minors, on the other hand, are limited to paying a maximum demand of $750 per incident, with a limit of three such awards per year. As was seen, foster or noncustodial parents are not civilly liable for retail thefts committed by foster or noncustodial children.

It should be noted here that the primary purpose of civil recovery laws is that they serve as a further deterrence to shoplifting. It is not their purpose that retail merchants should be made "whole" again. It is doubtful that such could be possible, given that most shoplifters are never caught and that civil recovery laws limit the amount of money that can be demanded. Indeed, states have passed merchant civil recovery laws in an attempt to give merchants another weapon that will hopefully deter or prevent individuals from shoplifting. The fact that merchants may recover some of the costs of their shoplifting prevention efforts is a benefit of the deterrent.

Stores that bring civil liability demands against shoplifters will hopefully recover some of the costs associated with the shoplifting problem. However, a store owner's demand for civil recovery from a shoplifter does not preclude the store owner from criminally prosecuting the shoplifter. Some are under the mistaken opinion that once shoplifters "pay" the civil demand notice, they are criminally off the hook. Nothing could be further from the truth. A store that presents a civil recovery demand to an individual may still pursue a prosecution against the individual.

What about the store that does not prosecute an individual for shoplifting? Can a store demand civil damages from a shoplifter even if the shoplifter was not convicted or, as is more likely to be the case, not prosecuted? The answer is yes. In fact, Alabama's law, like the law in most states, specifically allows that civil demand does not necessarily follow convictions for shoplifting. In other words, the law allows a retail merchant to place a civil demand against an individual for theft even if no charges against the individual were forthcoming. The only requisite for filing the civil demand note is that the individual took or was attempting to take retail merchandise without payment.

Alabama's law (AL ST §6-5-272) includes specific instructions on when civil demand may proceed and even provides the wording for a form letter that merchants are expected to send to the shoplifter as the basis of the civil demand.

> (a) A conviction or a plea of guilty to the criminal offense of theft of property as defined in Title 13A, Chapter 8, is not a prerequisite to the bringing of a civil suit, obtaining a judgment, or collecting that judgment under this article.

This part of the statute is clear in stating that the conviction of an individual for shoplifting (theft of property) is not a prerequisite for instituting a civil recovery effort against an individual under state law. A plea of guilty to a criminal offense is also not a requisite expectation before the filing of a civil demand letter can be commenced. In addition, the law allows that a civil recovery can be effected prior to a conviction or to the pleading of guilty by an offender.

The idea that a guilty plea or a conviction on theft charges must be obtained prior to sending out civil recovery letters is not unique to Alabama law. Indeed, most states' statutes have similar expectations. For instance, Oregon's civil recovery statute (OR.ST. § 30.875) explicitly states that "a conviction for theft under ORS 164.045 or 165.055 is not a condition precedent to the maintenance of a civil action under this section." In other words, merchants who pursue civil recovery under state civil recovery laws do not have to wait for a criminal conviction. Indeed, a conviction is not necessary to pursue damages under merchant civil recovery laws.

> (b) The fact that a merchant may bring a civil action against an individual as provided in this article shall not limit the right of the merchant to demand, in writing as set out in subsection (c)

below, that a person who is liable for damages and penalties under this article remit the damages and penalties prior to the consideration of the commencement of any legal action. (AL.ST. §6-5-272)

Subsection B of this statute allows that a retailer may seek civil damages prior to commencing court action. Such a civil recovery effort will take the form of a letter stating the cause of action and the amount of money the store seeks in recompense for the actions of the individual. The nice thing about this area of the statute is that it allows a merchant the right to send a letter to effect recovery without having to go, or prior to going, to court.

This provision of the law parallels such provisions of merchant statutes in other states. For instance, Oregon law stipulates, in part, that though the merchant may bring suit for damages under the law, that such a right does not "limit the right of the owner or the seller to demand, in writing, that a person who is liable for damages under this section remit said damages prior to the commencement of any legal action." Thus, stores may write civil demand letters, send them to shoplifters, and expect payment without the necessity of going through a civil court trial seeking damages allowed under the law.

Civil recovery laws, for the most part, are simple laws and include simple means by which a retailer can effect recovery. The simplicity of sending a letter stating that the individual is responsible to the retailer for a certain sum of money without resorting to the court system is the beauty of civil recovery statutes. It is expected that the letter will serve as the notice and effect recovery without further action on the part of the merchant.

By avoiding court, a merchant and the individual being sued are able to minimize their costs and, as such, minimize the imposition of time and effort on the merchant of a court showing. Merchants who successfully seek civil recovery and do so through a demand letter are able to receive recompense without the further cost or time considerations that a civil suit would normally entail.

Merchants have always been able to sue shoplifters for damages. Most have avoided such a course of action, since the amount of money that could be recovered under normal tort law usually was limited to the value of the item stolen. As such, court costs and attorney fees were often not recoverable. In addition, the time spent in court by the merchant made the practice of suing most shoplifters an uneconomic one.

(c) The demand letter must be prepared and include the following: On (insert date), you were apprehended for taking possession of, without paying for, merchandise belonging to (name of retailer/merchant). Under Alabama statute, a retailer/merchant is granted a civil cause of action against the person who intentionally deprives or intends to deprive a retailer/merchant of any merchandise without paying for it. The statute further provides that, separate from, and in addition to, any criminal action arising from your conduct, you may be held civilly liable for:

(a) Cost of merchandise, if damaged

(b) Expenses for the recovery of the merchandise of $200; and

(c) Court costs and reasonable attorney's fees.

This letter represents a demand from you for $(amount) as a means of satisfying this civil matter.

We do not wish to file a civil action against you. However, if we do not receive payment within 30 days from the date of this letter, we will make every effort to enforce our rights under this statute, which may include a civil court action.

Alabama's statute (AL.ST. §6-5-272) thoughtfully includes the basis for a demand letter filed pursuant to a shoplifting incident. As seen, the letter should clearly state that the state's law allows civil recovery for shoplifting. The letter should give notice that the individual is legally liable for costs surrounding the incident and state the amount of the dollar value sought for recompense. A civil recovery letter should state that the law allows for civil recovery in addition to or separate from any criminal action taken against the individual.

The letter should include a deadline for payment to be received by the store. Under Alabama law, the letter should state that payment needs to be made within 30 days from the date of the letter. Finally, the letter should emphasize that if payment is not forthcoming, the store will seek court action in enforcing the civil demand.

The statute shown is a statement of Alabama law. As such, its limits, the wording of the civil demand letter, and other factors should be followed by merchants operating in Alabama. In other states, merchants should be cognizant of their state's civil recovery law and act in accord with its provisions. Merchants in Alabama should prepare their civil demand letter in accord with the provisions of the state's statute. Merchants in other states need to assure that their letters meet the specifics of their states' laws.

Among the differences seen among the various states' statutes is the amount of money they allow a merchant to demand. For instance, in Oregon, the state's statute specifies that merchants may demand damages from shoplifters in the amount of the retail value of the merchandise not to exceed $500 plus a penalty to the owner of not less than $100 nor more than $250. California's civil recovery law concerning shoplifting allows merchants to collect up to $500 from someone caught shoplifting.

The law allows merchants to send civil demand letters to individuals regardless of whether or not those individuals have been found guilty of theft (shoplifting) or even whether criminal proceedings have been commenced against the individuals involved. Civil demand letters need to conform to state law. What happens when a civil demand letter is ignored or, more to the point, the individual, or in the case of a minor, the parents, refuse to pay the civil demand?

In a discussion with a store manager whose store has been sending civil demand letters for a few years, the manager made the observation that there were basically three types of responses to the civil demand letters sent out by her store. The three responses were quick and total payment, payment after further action, and no payment.

Obviously, the best kind of response one can hope for is one in which the individual who receives the civil demand letter pays the amount demanded, and pays it within the time frame allotted. The manager mentioned that about one-third of her store's demand letters had been quickly and appropriately responded to by the individuals. More often than not, the individuals responding quickly were parents or legal guardians of minors who wanted to put the incident behind them as quickly as possible. It was the manager's observation that these parents were sorry for their children's behavior, recognized that such behavior was wrong, and wanted to bring closure to the incident. As a consequence, they paid the civil demand letter without delay.

The second type of response the store manager noted was one in which the individual who received the letter did not reply in a timely manner. In such cases, which the store manager said accounted for about a third of her letters, a follow-up letter by the store's attorney, emphasizing that the store would be enforcing its civil demand through the court and again emphasizing the state's civil recovery statute, was usually sufficient to motivate the individuals in this group to pay. According to *Chain Store Age Executive* ("Loss Prevention," 1988), at least one private firm that pursues civil recovery on behalf of retailers reports that multiple letters are often needed to get individuals to pay.

Finally, the third type of response is the type to which every store manager can relate. These individuals are those who will not respond to the civil demand letter. Indeed, the store manager discussing her experiences noted that these individuals were generally among a class of people she described as destitute. They had no money with which to pay, and as a result, they could not pay even if they had a desire to do so, though most did not have such a desire. The manager noted that many of these appeared to be drug addicts or career criminals and had little inclination, if any, to pay for their offense. For this third group, she felt that further civil proceedings were usually not worth the effort. Given Ross Stores' reported 34 percent success rate, two-thirds of those who are contacted by Ross apparently do not pay anything.

A store that pursues civil demand needs to be aware that such a course of action will, if left to its logical conclusion, result in going to court to see that the rights of the retail merchant are enforced. Obviously, for those shoplifters who pay damages as specified in the demand letter, civil court proceedings will not ensue. For those who balk at paying or refuse to pay altogether, civil court proceedings will need to be pursued.

If civil court is relied upon to enforce a civil demand letter, then the court will want all evidence and documents related to the case. The bad news is that such reliance on the civil court system will cost the store in time, effort, and money. The good news is multifaceted. First, civil recovery laws allow the store to recoup legal fees and court costs related to the civil demand. Second, in cases of small demands, merchants can rely on small claims courts to pursue their rights.

Small claims courts, which are in existence in many jurisdictions, allow the easy pursuit of suits for damages up to a certain dollar limit. For instance, some jurisdictions allow claims for damages under $3,000 to be pursued in small claims courts. If a store in such a jurisdiction is pursuing a civil demand of, say, $750, then a small claims court may be the better choice as to how best to pursue its rights.

Again, evidence, perhaps in the form of testimony, and supporting documentation (a copy of the demand letter) will be a minimal expectation needed to support a store's claim. The decision as to whether to pursue a store's claim in small claims court, in regular district court, or perhaps not at all is best made with the advice and counsel of one's attorney.

According to those who pursue civil demand, good documentation is a must. Apprehension reports need to be well maintained and shoplifting incidents documented. Information contained in such reports needs to be accurate and correct. The name of the individual apprehended, the date, the specific merchandise stolen, the value of the merchandise involved, the address of the shoplifter, the phone number of the shoplifter (or the parent, if a minor), the names of witnesses, statements of witnesses, and other important information need to be recorded, documented, and filed in an orderly fashion.

The importance of a correct name and address cannot be overstated. Sending a civil demand letter to an address that does not exist does nothing to aid in the recovery of damages owed a merchant. If a merchant has to go to court, having all the pertinent information and adequate documentation to prove his or her case is imperative. If a retail merchant does not yet have an organized, systematic manner for collecting such information, then that merchant needs to implement such a system. As in all efforts that concern the law, documentation as to one's efforts is of paramount importance.

Civil demand laws do work. According to an article in *Chain Store Age Executive* ("Loss Prevention," 1988), Ross Stores relies on California's civil recovery law to collect monies from individuals it apprehends for shoplifting. The store reports that its program has had a 34 percent success rate, and in less than two years has raised approximately $75,000. The article mentions that parents are sometimes unaware that their children have been apprehended for shoplifting and that the letter is often the first they hear of such. Further, it is noted that shoplifting recidivism is low among those minors whose parents have received civil demand letters. Obviously, for many such parents, the price of their children committing shoplifting, a price the parents must pay, is too much to take lightly.

The success and impact of civil recovery laws on one drug retailer is indicative of what one may reasonably expect when a retailer seriously pursues civil recovery. Eckerd Drug Stores, a chain of 1,700 stores operating in the southeast United States, has taken a systematic approach to civil recovery. The store has reportedly generated in excess of $1 million through its civil recovery efforts, and reports an astonishing 55 percent recovery rate (Hartnett, 1994).

Civil recovery laws have gained in popularity to the point where their universal adoption has become a reality. The fifty states and the District of Columbia have enacted civil recovery laws. In addition, at least one Canadian jurisdiction has adopted a merchant civil recovery law. The popularity of pursuing civil recovery is gaining ground so fast that several firms have been established for the purpose of pursuing civil recovery for retailers who may be too busy to pursue such efforts on their own. Typically, these firms charge a percentage of the monies recovered and, in some cases, a fee for mailing expenses, for their efforts. Whether reliance for tracking and initiating civil recovery should be placed on an outside firm or on an employee is a cost-benefit question that can only be addressed on an individual store basis.

Civil recovery laws are laws. As such, merchants need to seek advice and counsel from their attorneys on how best to take advantage of their provisions. Legal counsel should also provide for the specific manner of writing the letter, given that the state statute has expectations and limitations as to what may be said and what may be demanded.

It can be argued that state legislatures have taken the needs of merchants to heart. Merchant protection statutes were enacted to provide merchants with civil liability immunity when merchants are found to be acting lawfully to protect their property rights. Merchants who know their state's merchant protection statute and act in accord with its provisions will be protected from civil suits arising from shoplifting apprehensions. Similarly, and as an adjunct to merchant protection statutes, legislatures have enacted civil recovery laws to allow merchants the right to be compensated easily for the costs associated with shoplifting. Again, merchants who know their state's civil recovery statute's provisions and act in accord with such provisions will find they are in the best position to take advantage of state law. Advice and counsel from the merchant's attorney on how best to take advantage of state law is a must.

Civil recovery laws have numerous benefits. They allow stores to recover money from individuals responsible for retail theft. They put the burden on shoplifters to help defray the costs of shoplifting and shoplifting prevention efforts. If successful, the costs of shoplifting would be borne ultimately by the thief, not by the general shopping public. Civil recovery laws have been credited with reducing the recidivism rate of juvenile offenders. Civil recovery laws are an excellent adjunct to the criminal laws to which shoplifters are subject. However, as most retail merchants are aware, criminal convictions of shoplifters seldom result in stiff penalties and often fail to serve as a significant deterrent. Criminal penalties coupled with civil recovery laws may likely do what neither was capable of doing alone; hopefully they will reduce shoplifting and the costs associated with the crime.

Civil recovery laws are simple. They allow merchants to write letters demanding recompense for damages they suffer from shoplifting. Civil recovery laws do not depend on a conviction for a criminal act to have an impact. Indeed, civil recovery laws stand on their own. Merchants need to be aware of civil recovery laws and their specifics, and work to take advantage of these laws to the benefit of their stores.

Table 6.1
Citation and Management Implications in Chapter Six

Case	Implication
Payless Drug Stores v. Brown, 708 P.2d 1143 (Or. 1985)	Civil recovery laws can be held to be constitutional. Arguments that civil recovery laws are vague, that parents should not be held liable for the actions of their children, that the amount allowed to be recovered under the law is unrelated to the amount of actual damages incurred by the store, and that civil recovery statutes violate the due process rights of individuals have not been recognized by the courts.

SUMMARY OF CONCEPTS IN CHAPTER SIX

1. Annually, shoplifting results in billions of dollars in lost merchandise sales and lost income.

2. Every state has enacted statutes that allow merchants to recover some of the costs associated with the shoplifting problem.

3. Civil recovery statutes empower merchants to seek recompense from persons caught shoplifting in their stores through the issuance of simple civil demand letters.

4. The wording of civil demand letters should adhere to the wording as specified in the civil recovery statute.

5. Civil demand letters that do not result in voluntary payment may have their intent enforced through the courts if necessary. A small claims court may be used to enforce the demand when the amount demanded falls within the court's purview and jurisdiction.

6. Civil recovery statutes typically allow merchants to recover the cost of the merchandise involved if it is damaged, a stipulated penalty fee, and reasonable attorney fees. Some states specify caps on the amounts that can be demanded.

7. Civil recovery statutes specify that parents are civilly liable for thefts committed by their minor children. While holding parents responsible, some states limit the liability exposure of parents.

8. Foster parents are exempted from civil recovery efforts for thefts committed by children placed in their care.

9. Not paying for a meal consumed at a restaurant is a form of theft and as such is covered by civil recovery statutes.

10. Civil recovery laws have as their primary purpose the deterrence of shoplifting.

11. Stores that actively pursue civil recovery may recover significant sums through such efforts.

12. A finding of guilty in a criminal trial is not a prerequisite to the filing of a civil demand. Indeed, civil demands may and often are pressed in the absence of a criminal prosecution.

13. A civil demand may precede a filing of criminal charges.

14. There are private firms that, for a fee, will pursue civil recovery on behalf of merchants.

15. An efficient civil demand effort requires adequate documentation and a systematic approach to handling the problem. Such an effort may prove economically beneficial.

Chapter Seven

Legal Avenues
and Alternatives

By now if one thing is not clear, it needs to be made clear here: the preparation and implementation of an effective shoplifting protection strategy involves an area of the law. It is an area of the law that merchants need to be aware of and appropriately respond to, given an increased willingness by individuals who feel they have been wronged to sue stores and others they feel are responsible. With large judgments against defendants becoming a costly fact of life despite the existence of merchant protection statutes, retail merchants need to be systematic and reasonable in their efforts directed at minimizing the shoplifting problem. Merchants need to recognize that merchant detention statutes and civil recovery statutes concern an area of the law, an area of the law for which one needs competent and current legal advice.

When choosing an attorney to advise management on shoplifting protection efforts, one needs to find an attorney who is experienced in commercial law. Choosing a divorce specialist is not sound practice unless one is contemplating a divorce. Since merchant protection statutes are embodied in state commercial law, a competent attorney with experience in commercial law is desired. Firms that do not currently have a competent legal advisor have three logical avenues to pursue in search of such counsel.

First, executives of firms that do not currently have legal counsel may check with other, noncompeting firms in the area for information on their experience with their outside attorneys and recommendations pursuant to their experience. Firsthand knowledge and experience can go a long way to make a case as to an attorney's qualifications and experience with commercial law. In checking with other executives, inquire as to the quality of service provided by the attorney and as to what types of problems their attorneys were especially adept at handling. Make it clear that an attorney with commercial law experience is desired.

Second, a search for attorneys with commercial law experience can be conducted at many libraries. Law libraries, most university libraries, and many public libraries carry the *Martindale-Hubbell Law Directory*. The *Directory* can usually be found in reference sections of those libraries that have acquired it. The *Directory* geographically lists the names of the great majority of attorneys practicing in the United States. Each attorney's reported area of specialty is listed along with any state-issued certification in a number of specialty areas. The *Martindale-Hubbell Law Directory* can be a good source for a listing of potential attorneys that a retail executive may wish to investigate further.

Finally, a retail executive desiring the services of an attorney with experience in commercial law can usually call the bar association headquartered in his or her state's capital. Most bar associations operate attorney referral services that will provide the names and contact information for attorneys fitting an explicit request parameter. When dealing with a referral service, one needs to be specific as to the type of attorney or the type of legal background and experience desired. Again, attorneys with commercial law experience, specifically retail trade experience, would be preferable in helping merchants plan shoplifting policy statements or civil recovery efforts. A bar's referral service can assist executives in filling such a need by directing them to such an attorney.

When choosing an attorney, one should narrow down choices and make an appointment to interview the attorneys that seem best able to fill one's needs. One should choose an attorney that makes one feel comfortable. The attorney should appear knowledgeable and answer reasonable questions posed by the interviewer. At such an interview, the attorney should preferably speak in the language of the layman, not in undecipherable legalese. If the attorney doesn't speak in a language and terminology that one can understand, can't answer basic questions about dealing with retail law, or doesn't make one feel comfortable, one should seek another candidate. A retail executive usually does not want an attorney who speaks about legal theories in a foreign language. One needs an attorney who is knowledgeable about retail laws, can put that knowledge to practical use, and can do so in a manner that is understandable by the client.

In addition to knowledge of retail law, when one can acquire an attorney who is knowledgeable about contract law, unfair trade practice acts, employment law, disability law, and other laws that may be relevant to one's specific business, then that attorney is in a position to offer the retail merchant an even better level of legal counsel and more comprehensive legal services. Establishing a good business relationship with one's attorney is a good business practice. Such a relationship, coupled with an understanding of one's business and retail trade laws, will aid in one's planning for the development of effective shoplifting protection efforts.

Having an attorney in on the planning process from the beginning is paramount in the effort to adequately protect one's property rights. It is cheap assurance that the firm will be following both a practical and a legal course of action aimed at providing reasonable security for property. A competent attorney can help make sure that the firm continues to follow the intent as well as the specifics of the law.

It cannot be emphasized enough that merchant protection statutes and civil recovery statutes are state laws. As such, there are differences in the various states' versions of merchant protection statutes and civil recovery statutes, some of which were discerned in the cases cited. Additionally, other laws that often enter into discussions involving civil liability and civil recovery are frequently state laws and vary widely as to their specifics. Due to the differences among the states' statutes and changes in laws over time, it is important that a firm seeking protection of its property rights and recompense for its efforts pursue competent legal advice in the geographic area or areas in which it operates.

Finally, the cases included in this book are typical cases involving merchant protection statutes and civil recovery efforts and are presented for explanatory purposes. They do not represent all of the cases nor all of the potential circumstances under which a store may reasonably pursue its property rights or under which a claim for damages may be negated or pursued. For that reason, they and the plan in this book need to be used as a foundation for understanding shoplifting laws, their scope, and their impact. Such an understanding should be used as the basis for discussions with one's legal counsel and for management to begin its efforts to adequately protect its property rights. The analyses of the cases presented in this book and the action plan as recommended should not be construed as legal advice. That is the role one's attorney plays, and as such, the necessity for competent legal counsel in preparations centering around protecting one's property cannot be overstated.

A final alternative to actually going to court is settling a case prior to the court date. While this may not be of interest to one or both parties, such is often a cheaper method, and if the case is settled in a just manner, may prove more advantageous to both parties than pursuing the action in court. Advice from legal counsel can aid clients in a settlement resolution. Knowledgeable advice as to when to settle and when not to is needed in such circumstances. The practice of settling out of court is often an economic one. As the court noted in *Abba Rubber Company v. Seaquist* (a non-shoplifting-related case), "litigation is extraordinarily expensive." Settling an issue out of court is usually preferable to going to court and having the issue settled there. One's attorney is in the best position to advise on such an effort.

And finally, the issues revolving around merchant protection statutes and civil recovery statutes are legal issues. Despite such, it is not the intent of this book to prepare one to go to court. Taking a case to court will consume much time, interfere with ongoing operations, and be costly; further, it is just plain nerve wracking. If court can be avoided and one's property maintained, significant benefits to the retailer will ensue. The intent of the protection plan discussed is to emphasize that if one develops a proper protection plan and follows the law, one may not be as likely to have to pursue one's rights in court. Hopefully, one's property will be secure and merchant protection statutes will provide the protection they offer.

The problem of retail crime is so costly and so ubiquitous that it will probably surprise few to learn that retailers have often banded together to fight the threat. Shopping center merchant membership organizations often act as a group in preparing antishoplifting literature and training programs in order to prepare their stores' employees to deal more effectively with the problem. Merchants have come together to discuss methods and hire security guards to minimize the impact that retail crime can inflict on the unprepared. The question arises, though, whether merchants who band together with the purpose of minimizing shoplifting in a center garner the protection that merchant protection statutes offer. It appears that as long as such affiliations result in lawful actions and as long as they do not encourage unlawful actions, such efforts can be construed to be privileged.

A case in point is the case of *Dangberg v. Sears, Roebuck & Company*. In *Dangberg*, Dangberg sought damages she claimed were incurred as a result of an alleged civil conspiracy in which a Sears employee played a part. She sought damages for slander and damages for false imprisonment. It was claimed that the false imprisonment and slander occurred as the result of an alleged civil conspiracy entered into between an employee of a Sears store and employees of an adjacent store.

Information on this Nebraska case indicates that employees of a Sears store and a J. C. Brandeis & Sons store, located adjacent to one another in an Omaha shopping center, did meet and discuss mutual concerns as they related to minimizing the shoplifting problem. It was alleged that at one such meeting, the Sears employee mentioned that Dangberg was a frequent shopper at the center, that she often carried large bags of merchandise, and that as a consequence, based on his experience, he suspected Dangberg might be a potential shoplifter. Reportedly, he stated that he had never caught Dangberg shoplifting, but that based on his experience with shoplifters and Dangberg's habit of carrying large bags, he was concerned. Further, the Sears employee mentioned that he had observed Dangberg often moving between the two stores. As a result of his statement, a Brandeis store employee asked that the Sears employee alert his store anytime Dangberg was spotted leaving Sears and entering his store. The Sears employee agreed to do so.

Some days later, Dangberg was spotted in the Sears store. She purportedly made no purchase and then proceeded through the store and walked into the Brandeis store. The Sears employee, as agreed, called the Brandeis store and alerted that store's management to the fact that Dangberg had left the Sears store moments earlier and was now on the premises of the Brandeis store. A Brandeis security guard was alerted to the fact that Dangberg was in the store. The guard followed Dangberg as she left the store and walked to a nearby bus stop. Once there, the guard approached Dangberg, identified himself, and asked that she return to the store so that he might search her purse and bag. Purportedly, others at the bus stop heard the guard's comments; hence there was a charge of slander. The guard's actions relative to the detention were the basis for Dangberg's charges of false imprisonment. Dangberg felt that she had been maliciously slandered and believed that the guard's actions had been initiated without probable cause.

Testimony indicated that the only action taken by the Sears employee was alerting the Brandeis store employees to the fact that Dangberg had entered their store. The Sears employee did not accuse Dangberg of stealing. The Sears employee had not initiated the apprehension, nor had he encouraged it. He had not accused Dangberg of committing a crime, nor had he seen Dangberg commit a crime. In short, the Sears employee had nothing to do with the detention.

The court noted that the agreement of stores' employees to watch Dangberg closely in an attempt to catch her in a criminal act (shoplifting) was not unlawful. A civil conspiracy had not been entered into between the employees of the two stores. The two had not conspired to accomplish an unlawful action, nor had they conspired to accomplish some lawful effort through unlawful means. Hence the Sears employee had not conducted an illegal activity. The discussion between the two stores' employees was deemed a privileged communication related to their legitimate joint efforts and interest in reducing shoplifting in their stores.

In short, the Sears employee was privileged to discuss joint efforts to deter shoplifting. The employee said he had never caught Dangberg stealing; it was just that her habit of carrying large shopping bags made him suspect that she might be shoplifting. The Sears employee did not accuse Dangberg of shoplifting the day the Brandeis guard apprehended Dangberg. The Sears employee brought her presence in the Brandeis store to the attention of management. He did not encourage her apprehension. He did not participate in the detention. The Sears employee did not slander Dangberg. The trial court's finding for the Sears store was affirmed by the Supreme Court of Nebraska.

The question arises regularly as to what to do when probable cause exists to detain only one of two or more people who may be shopping together. This is a question to address with one's attorney. However, the answer typically is that when probable cause exists to stop an individual who may be a part of a group and a detention is to follow, the person for whom probable cause exists to detain is the person on whom the investigation should turn, and that is the person who should be detained. Granted, in many such incidents, others in a shopping party may elect to or insist on staying. However, it is important to remember that merchant detention statutes offer merchants a privilege to detain individuals only when probable cause exists to believe they are shoplifting merchandise or have shoplifted merchandise. If probable cause exists to believe that two or more people are working together to steal retail merchandise, then the privilege to conduct a reasonable investigation should apply to the two or more people for which probable cause exists. If probable cause exists to detain one individual in a group and a merchant elects to detain others in the group for which probable cause does not exist, then a store may find itself vulnerable even with the protection offered by merchant detention statutes.

In the case of *Kneas v. The Hecht Company*, two young teenagers, Kneas and Lohmeier, entered a Hecht Company store located in Silver Spring, Maryland. While shopping in the store for a jacket, Lohmeier was observed by two store detectives taking a small cross worth approximately one dollar and concealing it on his person, according to testimony. The store detectives detained the two youths and, after questioning, turned them over to the police for further processing. The juvenile branch of the police department concluded that Lohmeier was guilty of shoplifting but that accusations that Kneas was involved were unfounded. Accordingly, no further action was initiated against Kneas, and he was released. Since he was only thirteen, Kneas's father filed suit against the Hecht Company claiming that his son had been falsely arrested and falsely imprisoned.

The civil trial against the Hecht Company store went as some might expect. The jury found against the store. Kneas was awarded $10,000 in compensatory damages by the jury. Ostensibly, the jury believed that the store's actions against Kneas, which were not based on probable cause, had been conducted in such a manner as to merit the awarding of punitive damages. Kneas was awarded $30,000 in punitive damages by the jury.

At the announcement of the jury award, the store asked for a directed verdict in its favor, contending that no evidence had been presented that would logically support the awarding of compensatory or punitive damages. The trial judge reserved his decision under Maryland law. In addition, the store sought a ruling in the store's favor notwithstanding the verdict or, in the alternative, a new trial. The store claimed it should have received a directed verdict due to the ex-

LEGAL AVENUES AND ALTERNATIVES 149

cessiveness of the awards and errors committed by the court in delivering instructions to the jury.

Three months later, the trial judge concluded that since the existence of malice on the part of the store had not been proven, the awarding of punitive damages and the instructions to the jury as to the possibility of awarding punitive damages had been in error. Accordingly, he granted the motion for judgment notwithstanding the verdict on the awarding of punitive damages, with the proviso that should his ruling be overturned by the appellate court, a new trial would ensue. In addition, the judge found the compensatory damages had been excessive and reduced the compensatory award to $5,000.

In short, as the civil trial indicates, probable cause should be at the heart of each detention. If probable cause to detain does not exist as it applies to a particular individual, then that individual should not be detained. To do otherwise opens the store to the possibility of paying damages.

Another aspect of this case that is of interest is that in making the reduction to $5,000, the trial judge exercised his discretion by making the $5,000 a take-it-or-leave-it proposition. In other words, the plaintiff could take the $5,000 as compensation and everything would end; there would be no further appeal. Alternatively, the plaintiff could forego the $5,000 and continue to pursue damages as well as a new trial. The judge allowed Kneas's family one week to decide if the $5,000 was acceptable. Apparently, the $5,000 was deemed acceptable. The funds were paid, and the attorney for Kneas filed a notice with the clerk directing that the judgment be marked "paid, settled and satisfied."

An appeal on the finding relative to punitive damages was filed. The Court of Appeals of Maryland found that the trial judge had not exceeded his authority in the handling of the case. The appellate court noted that the plaintiff forfeited his right to a further review by his own actions (in accepting the $5,000 and ordering the clerk to mark the judgment "paid, settled and satisfied." It is well established that one cannot accept the benefits of a judgment and later seek to question its validity. The court noted that once Kneas accepted the $5,000 as adequate compensation for the incident in lieu of seeking a new trial, a proposition within the discretion of the trial judge, the entire litigation came to a conclusion. There would be no further deliberations pursuant to damages allegedly incurred by Kneas. The appeal by Kneas was dismissed.

Although Kneas was limited to only the $5,000 award in his effort to receive recompense for damages, it should be noted that had probable cause to detain him existed, he probably would have received nothing. A store should not apprehend and detain persons for whom probable cause is not known to exist. It is imperative that a store manager seek the advice of competent legal counsel when establishing shoplifting policy statements. Legal counsel should be relied upon to explain the concept of probable cause and its importance as a basis for the actions of store employees.

In the case of *Gatto v. Publix Supermarket, Inc.*, Gatto sought damages for assault and battery, false imprisonment, and malicious prosecution. Testimony revealed that the incident surrounded Gatto's apprehension by Publix employees in which Gatto's hand was touched by the employees as they attempted to retrieve paperback books from Gatto. Subsequently, the store employees called police and preferred charges against him. The prosecution of Gatto for shoplifting was dropped, and he filed civil suit seeking damages. The store requested directed verdicts on all counts, noting that the actions of its employees were based on probable cause. The trial court granted the directed verdicts for the store. Gatto appealed the directed verdicts.

On appeal, the appellate court noted that Gatto's own testimony indicated that he felt he was free to leave at any time. There was no evidence to indicate that Gatto had been placed in fear or that the touching of his hand had caused harm to him. Store employees testified that they called police at Gatto's insistence. Given this and other factors, the court ruled that the evidence did not support Gatto's claims of false imprisonment or assault and battery. On the malicious prosecution count, though, the appellate court noted that the fact that Gatto's prosecution was dropped by authorities might indicate that he had been the victim of a malicious prosecution. The appellate court affirmed the lower court's verdicts on the false imprisonment and assault and battery claims, but reversed the directed verdict on the charge of malicious prosecution and ordered a trial on that charge.

The instructions given to the jury in the case of *Dawson v. Pay Less Shoes, Inc.* were the basis of the appeal by the plaintiff. In *Dawson*, it was argued that the instructions requested by the store and delivered by the court to the jury had been in error. The instructions were essentially three paragraphs. The first two paragraphs simply quoted parts of Arkansas's merchant detention statute. Paragraph one of the instructions stated that the concealment upon a "person or the person of another, of unpurchased goods or merchandise offered for sale by any store or other business establishment shall give rise to a presumption that the actor took goods with the purpose of depriving the owner, or another person, having an interest therein." The statement allows one to assume that if an individual is concealing goods, then it is likely that the individual is concealing the goods with the intent to deprive the merchant of his or her property.

The second paragraph in the contested instructions concerned detentions arising out of the presumption associated with the willful concealment of goods. The statement allowed that a person "may be detained in a reasonable manner and for a reasonable length of time by

a peace officer or a merchant or a merchant's employee in order that recovery of such goods may be effected." Further, the statement concluded that such a detention does not render the peace officer or
merchant "criminally or civilly liable for false arrest, false imprisonment, or unlawful detention."

The third paragraph in the instructions was the source of the majority of the contention arising from the instructions. The third paragraph
said that if the jury were to find that the plaintiff had "concealed unpurchased goods or merchandise upon her person, then the defendant's
employee and the police were entitled to detain her in a reasonable
manner for a reasonable length of time" and the verdict of the jury
should be for the store.

The appellate court noted that the first two paragraphs were quotes
from the state's merchant detention law, and as such were not prejudicial, nor were they inappropriate, given the case. Indeed, the wording
of the first two paragraphs was proper and applicable to the facts of the
case. Finally, the court noted that the third paragraph of the instructions was not prejudicial and had been proper. The court found that the
instructions merely stated that the jury should find for the store only
if the jury found that the plaintiff had concealed upon her person
merchandise that had not been purchased. Such a finding would be
statutorily based, since the state's law allowed the presumption of
shoplifting, given concealment of unpurchased goods. In short, the appellate court found that the instructions did not impact on the evidence
in the case, but rather were appropriate instructions on state law pursuant to the nature of the case.

In summary, merchant detention statutes and civil recovery laws are
state laws. They vary in their specifics among the states, and laws
change even within a state over time. A merchant desiring to address
the problem of shoplifting needs to take an affirmative stance to address the problem. It is recommended that a store have a written policy
based on the law, and the policy should detail how shoplifting apprehensions and detentions will be handled. Employees should be required
to know their store policy and expected to follow its specifics. It is a
good idea to have legal counsel in on the policy statement development,
as one is dealing with an area of law. Detentions should not be initiated
without probable cause to believe a crime is being commited or has
been commited. Detentions need to be reasonable in the manner in
which they are conducted and need to be for no longer than a reasonable period of time. Merchants need to take advantage of civil recovery
laws. Civil recovery laws are proving to be a major asset to retailers
and a major deterrent to shoplifting. Finally, merchants need to take
the problem seriously. Shoplifting is the costliest crime impacting retailers. It will take a concerted effort to protect the property interests
of retail merchants and minimize the impact of shoplifting.

Table 7.1
Citations and Management Implications in Chapter Seven

Case	Implication
Abba Rubber Company v. Seaquist, 286 Cal.Rptr. 518 (Cal.App. 4Dist. 1991)	Litigation can be extraordinarily expensive. Settling out of court may be preferable. Legal counsel is in the best position to so advise.
Dangberg v. Sears, Roebuck & Company, 252 N.W.2d 168 (Neb. 1977)	Lawfully discussing shoplifting detention efforts with others does not result in a loss of privilege. A merchant who does not assist in another merchant's detention does not assume liability.
Kneas v. The Hecht Company, 262 A.2d 518 (Md.App. 1970)	Stop only individuals for whom probable cause exists to indicate they are shoplifting or have shoplifted. The fact that a store employee possesses probable cause to detain one individual should not give rise to the belief that someone else who is in that person's company is shoplifting.
Gatto v. Publix Supermarket, Inc., 387 So.2d 377 (Fla.App. 1980)	Probable cause to initiate a detention is not necessarily the level of probable cause to support a prosecution. It is not necessary to have a successful prosecution to have cause to detain for investigatory purposes.
Dawson v. Pay Less Shoes, Inc., 598 S.W.2d 83 (Ark. 1980)	Instructions to the jury that merely communicate state law and that do not weigh on the evidence can be appropriate.

SUMMARY OF CONCEPTS IN CHAPTER SEVEN

1. As in any situation involving the law, obtain legal counsel from the start.

2. In choosing an attorney, choose one who has commercial law expertise and who communicates well.

3. Pursuing a court case can be costly. Rely on the advice of competent counsel in dealing with legal issues.

4. Merchant detention statutes and civil recovery statutes are state laws. Their specifics vary among the states and can vary within a state over time.

5. Since merchant protection statutes and civil recovery statutes are state laws, a management strategy dealing with related issues should have input from one's legal counsel.

6. Merchants who act cooperatively may enjoy civil liability immunity when they are acting on probable cause and in a reasonable manner.

7. Merchants should detain only those individuals for whom they possess probable cause to believe are committing a retail theft or have committed a retail theft. Detaining individuals without probable cause will expose the merchant to civil liability.

8. Court instructions to juries that merely restate the state's merchant detention statute and that are not prejudicial are proper.

9. Normally, in situations where the existence of probable cause is in dispute, a jury will decide on its existence.

Appendix:
Legal Cases Cited

Abba Rubber Company v. Seaquist, 286 Cal.Rptr. 518 (Cal.App. 4Dist. 1991)

Bartolo v. Boardwalk Regency Hotel Casino, Inc., 449 A.2d 1339 (N.J.Super.L. 1982)

Bishop v. Bockoven, Inc. and Metropolitan Protection Service, Inc., 260 N.W.2d 433 (Neb. 1977)

Black v. Clark's Greensboro, Inc., 139 S.E.2d 199 (N.C. 1964)

Bonkowski v. Arlan's Department Store, 162 N.W.2d 347 (Mich.App. 1968)

Bryant v. Sears, Roebuck & Company, 25 ATLA L.Rep. 271

Castaneda v. J. C. Penney, Inc., 438 S.W.2d 938 (Tex.App. 1969)

Causey v. Katz & Bestoff, Inc., 539 So.2d 944 (La.App. 4Cir. 1989)

Cervantez v. J. C. Penney Company, Inc., 595 P.2d 975 (Cal. 1979)

Chelette v. Wal-Mart Stores, Inc., 535 So.2d 558 (La.App. 3Cir. 1988)

City of Pensacola v. Owens, 369 So.2d 238 (Fla. 1979)

City Stores Company v. Gibson, 263 A.2d 252 (D.C.App. 1970)

Clark v. I. H. Rubenstein, Inc., 25 ATLA No.1 (1982)

Clifton v. Richman Gordman, Inc. and Horan, 215 N.W.2d 105 (Neb. 1974)

Coblyn v. Kennedy's, Inc., 268 N.E.2d 860 (Mass. 1971)

Conn v. Paul Harris Stores, Inc., 439 N.E.2d 195 (Ind.App. 1982)

Cooke v. J. J. Newberry & Company, 232 A.2d 425 (N.J. 1967)

Dangberg v. Sears, Roebuck & Company, 252 N.W.2d 168 (Neb. 1977)

Dawson v. Pay Less Shoes, Inc., 598 S.W.2d 83 (Ark. 1980)

DeMarie v. Jefferson Stores, Inc., 442 So.2d 1014 (Fla.App. 3Dist. 1983)

Dent v. May Department Stores Company, 459 A.2d 1042 (D.C.App. 1982)

Eason v. J. Weingarten, Inc., 219 So.2d 516 (La.App. 3Cir. 1969)

Gabrou v. May Department Stores Company, 462 A.2d 1102 (D.C.App. 1983)

Gaszak v. Zayre of Illinois, Inc., 305 N.E.2d 704 (ILL.App. 1Dist. 1973)

Gatto v. Publix Supermarket, Inc., 387 So.2d 377 (Fla.App. 1980)

Gibson Discount Center, Inc. v. Cruz, 562 S.W.2d 511 (Tex.App. 1978)

Gibson's Products, Inc. v. Edwards, 247 S.E.2d 183 (Ga.App. 1978)

Godwin v. Gibson Products Company of Albany, Inc., 172 S.E.2d 467 (Ga.App. 1970)

Gonzales v. Harris, 528 P.2d 259 (Colo.App. 1974)

Hales v. McCrory-McLellan Corporation, 133 S.E.2d 225 (N.C. 1963)

Hardin v. Barker's of Monroe, Inc., 336 So.2d 1031 (La.App. 1976)

Huskinson v. Vanderheiden, 251 N.W.2d 144 (Neb. 1977)

Jefferson Stores, Inc. v. Caudell, 228 So.2d 99 (Fla.App. 3Dist. 1969)

Johnson v. Bloomingdale's, 420 N.Y.S.2d 840 (N.Y.S. 1979)

Johnson v. Schwegmann Brothers, Inc., 397 So.2d 868 (La.App. 4Cir. 1981)

Jorgensen v. Skaggs, 668 P.2d 565 (Utah 1983)

Kneas v. The Hecht Company, 262 A.2d 518 (Md.App. 1970)

Lansburgh's, Inc. v. Ruffin, 372 A.2d 561 (D.C.App. 1977)

Lerner Shops of Nevada, Inc. v. J. P. Marin, 423 P.2d 398 (Nev. 1967)

Lipari v. Volume Shoe Corporation, 664 S.W.2d 953 (Mo.App. 1983)

Mahon v. King's Department Store, Inc., 25 ATLA L.Rep. 31

Mapes v. National Food Stores of Louisiana, Inc., 329 So.2d 831 (La.App. 1Cir. 1976)

Martinez v. Goodyear Tire & Rubber Company, 651 S.W.2d 18 (Tex.App. 4Dist. 1983)

Montgomery Ward & Company, Inc. v. Keulemans, 340 A.2d 705 (Md.App. 1975)

Moore v. Target Stores, Inc., 571 P.2d 1236 (Okla.App. 1977).

Murray v. Wal-Mart, Inc., 874 F.2d 555 (8th Cir. 1989)

Parker v. Sears, Roebuck & Company, 418 So.2d 1361 (La.App. 1982)

Payless Drug Stores v. Brown, 708 P.2d 1143 (Or. 1985)

People v. Lee, 204 Cal.Rptr. 667 (Cal.Super. 1984)

Robinson v. Wieboldt Stores, Inc., 433 N.E.2d 1005 (Ill.App. 1982)

Rusnak v. Giant Foods, Inc., 337 A.2d 445 (Md.S.App. 1975)

Safeway Stores, Inc. v. Gross, 398 S.W.2d 669 (Ark. 1966)

Safeway Stores, Inc. v. Kelly, 448 A.2d 856 (D.C.App. 1982)

Schmidt v. Richman Gordman, Inc. and Horan, 215 N.W.2d 105 (Neb. 1974)

Schwane v. Kroger Company, Inc., 480 S.W.2d 113 (Mo.App. 1972)

Shaw v. Rose's Stores, Inc. and R. M. Faw, 205 S.E.2d 789 (N.C.App. 1974)

Solomon v. United States, 559 F.2d 309 (5th Cir. 1977)

Southwest Drug Stores of Mississippi, Inc. v. Garner, 195 So.2d 837 (Miss. 1967)

Swift v. S. S..Kresge Company, Inc., 284 S.E.2d 74 (Ga.App. 1981)

Taylor v. Dillard's Department Stores, Inc., 971 F.2d 601 (10th Cir. 1992)

Tweedy v. J. C. Penney Company, Inc., 221 S.E.2d 152 (Va. 1976)

Wal-Mart Stores, Inc. v. Yarbrough, 681 S.W.2d 359 (Ark. 1984)

Weissman v. K-Mart Corporation, 396 So.2d. 1164 (Fla. 3DCA 1981)

West v. Wal-Mart Stores, Inc., 539 So.2d 1258 (La.App. 3Cir. 1989)

Williams v. F. W. Woolworth Company, 242 So.2d 16 (La.App. 4Cir. 1970)

Wilson v. Wal-Mart Stores, Inc., 525 So.2d 11 (La.App. 3Cir. 1988)

W. T. Grant Company v. Guercio, 238 A.2d 855 (Md.App. 1968)

References

Alabama's Laws on Worthless Checks. *Shoplifting and Civil Recovery for Theft of Merchandise*, 1996. Office of the Alabama Attorney General and Alabama Retail Association.

Arey, N., and A. R. Tays. 1994. "Drug Arrest Stuns Tennis World, Celeb Watchers." *Atlanta Constitution*, May 18, G1.

Berstein, Paul. 1985. "Cheating—the New National Pastime." *Business*, October/November/December, 24–33.

Budden, Michael C. 1984. "Store Managers and Shoplifting: An Empirical Analysis." *Small Business Institute Review,* Summer, 71–75.

Budden, Michael C., Joseph H. Miller, Jr., and Tom F. Griffin III. 1996. "A Large-Scale Test of the Biorhythm-Shoplifting Connection Hypothesis." *Psychology & Marketing*, May, 321–29.

Budden, Michael C., Joseph H. Miller, Jr., and John W. Yeargain. 1991. "Strategies for Dealing with Shoplifting: A Managerial and Legal Perspective." *American Business Review,* January, 28–40.

Budden, Michael C., Joseph H. Miller, Jr., John W. Yeargain, and Renee Culverhouse. 1991. "Merchant Protection Statutes: Management Safety Nets or Tightropes." *Journal of Managerial Issues,* Spring, 62–76.

Budden, Michael C., and John W. Yeargain. 1986. "Preventing Shoplifting without Being Sued." *Business Forum,* Summer, 8–11.

Canton, Lucien G. 1987. "Should Shoplifters Be Prosecuted?" *Security Management*, May, 61–64.

Crowley, Carolyn Hughes. 1996. "A Civil Alternative." *The Washington Post*, May 21, B5.

Dacy II, J. 1994. "When Shoplifters Ask for Refunds." *Nation's Business*, 27.

Dowling, Claudia Glenn. 1988. "Shoplifting." *Life*, August, 33–38.

Ecenbarger, William. 1996. "They're Stealing You Blind." *Reader's Digest*, June, 97–103.

"Employee Theft Hurts Retailers." 1992. *Christian Science Monitor*, January 27, 1.

Espinosa, Douglas C. 1989. "Shoplifters: No Sale." *Security Management*, May, 64–68.

Faria, Anthony J. 1977. "Minimizing Shoplifting Losses: Some Practical Guidelines." *Journal of Small Business Management,* October, 37–44.

Greenberg, Jerald. 1990. "Employee Theft as a Reaction to Underpayment Inequity." *Journal of Applied Psychology*, October, 561–568.

Griffin, Roger. 1988. "The Civil Recovery System: Saving the Bottom Line." *Non-Foods Merchandising*, April, 19.

Hartnett, Michael. 1994. "Paying the Price of Crime." *Stores*, December, 48.

Hayes, Read. 1990. "Winning the Civil Recovery War." *Security Management*, March, 83–84

———. 1992. "The Civil Recovery Side of Shoplifting." *Security Management*, March, 30–32.

Hollinger, Richard C., Dean A. Dabney, Gang Lee, and Read Hayes. "1997 National Retail Security: Final Report." University of Florida, Gainesville, FL.

Klokis, Holly. 1985. "Confessions of an Ex-Shoplifter—When You Least Expect It." *Chain Store Age Executive*, February, 15–18.

"Loss Prevention Can Be Profitable." 1988. *Chain Store Age Executive*, December, 12–13.

Ohlhausen, Peter. 1987. "Keep Those Sticky Fingers Clean." *Security Management*, March, 40–44.

"Police Presence—Life Size Police Dummies Foil Shoplifters." 1990. *Time*, June 8, 53.

Ryan, Patrick. 1974. "The Hard Sell Also Entices Shoplifters." *Smithsonian*, October, 140.

Schmitt, E. 1993. "Acting Army Secretary Accused of Shoplifting, Is Placed On Leave." *The New York Times*, August 28, A6.

"Shoplifting Challenges Retailers." 1992. *Christian Science Monitor*, December 9, 7.

Sloane, L. 1991. "Devices that Try to Outwit Shoplifters." *The New York Times*, August 24, A52.

Stinson, Delany J. 1988. "Attention Retailers: Civil Law Provides a Tonic." *Security Management*, September, 129–32.

"To Catch a Thief." 1988. *Non-Foods Merchandising*, April, 15–20.

"Wanamaker Keeps Tabs On Loss." 1987. *Chain Store Age Executive*, July, 102–103.

Williams, Hubert, Brian Forst, and Edwin E. Hamilton. 1988. "Stop: Should You Arrest That Person?" *Security Management*, September, 52–58.

"Worker Theft Imposes Rising Cost on Retailers and Customers." 1990. *The Wall Street Journal*, February 20, A1.

"World Wire: Crime Crimps U.K. Shopkeepers." 1994. *The Wall Street Journal*, January 19, A15.

Index

About the Author

MICHAEL CRAIG BUDDEN, Ph.D., is Dean of the College of Business, Southeastern Louisiana University. In addition to many publications in a variety of journals, he has written *Protecting Trade Secrets Under the Uniform Trade Secrets Act: Practical Advice for Executives* (Quorum, 1996).